Target Underwear and

a Vera Wang Gown

Target Underwear and a Vera Wang Gown

Notes from
a Single Girl's Closet

Adena Halpern

GOTHAM BOOKS

Although some names and identifying characteristics of the people in this memoir have been changed to protect their privacy, all references to clothing remain unchanged . . . no matter how humiliating it looked.

GOTHAM BOOKS
Published by Penguin Group (USA) Inc.
375 Hudson Street, New York, New York 10014, U.S.A.
Penguin Group (Canada), 90 Eglinton Avenue East, Suite 700, Toronto, Ontario M4P 2Y3, Canada (a division of Pearson Penguin Canada Inc.); Penguin Books Ltd, 80 Strand, London WC2R 0RL, England; Penguin Ireland, 25 St Stephen's Green, Dublin 2, Ireland (a division of Penguin Books Ltd); Penguin Group (Australia), 250 Camberwell Road, Camberwell, Victoria 3124, Australia (a division of Pearson Australia Group Pty Ltd); Penguin Books India Pvt Ltd, 11 Community Centre, Panchsheel Park, New Delhi - 110 017, India; Penguin Group (NZ), cnr Airborne and Rosedale Roads, Albany, Auckland 1310, New Zealand (a division of Pearson New Zealand Ltd); Penguin Books (South Africa) (Pty) Ltd, 24 Sturdee Avenue, Rosebank, Johannesburg 2196, South Africa

Penguin Books Ltd, Registered Offices: 80 Strand, London WC2R 0RL, England

Published by Gotham Books, a division of Penguin Group (USA) Inc.

First printing, July 2006
10   9   8   7   6   5   4   3   2   1

Gotham Books and the skyscraper logo are trademarks of Penguin Group (USA) Inc.

LIBRARY OF CONGRESS CATALOGING-IN-PUBLICATION DATA
Halpern, Adena.
Target underwear and a Vera Wang gown : notes from a single girl's closet / by Adena Halpern.
p.   cm.
ISBN 1-592-40221-6
1. Women's clothing—psychological aspects.   2. Clothing and dress—Psychological aspects.
3. Fashion—Psychological aspects.   I. Title.
GT1720.H35 2006
391'.2—dc22   2005044792

Printed in the United States of America
Set in Berkeley Book with ChaletComprime-MilanSixty
Designed by Sabrina Bowers

While the author has made every effort to provide accurate telephone numbers and Internet addresses at the time of publication, neither the publisher nor the author assumes any responsibility for errors, or for changes that occur after publication. Further, publisher does not have any control over and does not assume any responsibility for author or third-party Web sites or their content.

For my mom and dad

Contents

Contents

Target Underwear and

a Vera Wang Gown

Introduction:
If I Had a Closet

Sometimes I wish that rather than photo albums or scrap-books, I had a closet full of every piece of clothing that meant anything in my life.

Looking from the left of the closet, I'd find my grandmother's mink coat, a broken strand of faux pearls in the pocket that she'd smashed when she and my grandfather had gotten too wild in their salsa dancing. Next to the mink would be a perfectly pre-served gray flannel suit of my grandfather's with a perfectly folded handkerchief in the pocket. Next to their section, I'd have the steel blue, circa-1970s Oscar de la Renta gown of my mother's, a Louis Vuitton bucket bag, and a cream-colored tailored suit—those classic styles that always make her look timeless. I'd have my dad's white doctor's coat, a stethoscope hanging out of the right pocket, and I'd think about how important and serious he looked when I visited him at the hospital. Next to the doctor's coat would be his well-worn blue sweatsuit, the one with the permanent pizza stains on the jacket that he'd put on the second he got home. That sweatsuit always meant playtime. I'd have my brother David's varsity wrestling jacket and brother Michael's varsity cross-country jacket to remember the feeling of being the awkward little sister who thought her older brothers were the coolest, strongest, and most popular boys in high school, but would never let them know.

I'd take out my college sweetheart's eighties 8-ball jacket and lay my old Madonna wannabe bustier and leggings next to it and reminisce about that feeling of first-time true love. I'd even have my Girbaud orange-neon-colored parachute pants next to a pair of split Dolphin shorts, those major fashion faux pas that at the time seemed the height of fabulous and only now follow the words "I can't believe I ever wore that!"

My friend Susan is always amazed when I can immediately tell her what anyone was wearing at significant moments. Susan, for example, was wearing a pink Betsey Johnson Lycra flowered dress with a ruffled collar when I first met her, an outfit that I later borrowed. Heidi was wearing a pair of blue-and-white-striped drawstring pants and a white T-shirt. Rachel wore a three-quarter-length black suit jacket on her first day at her big new job. Amy wore a pair of white leggings and a long white T-shirt hiked up on the right side with a banana clip the day we graduated from high school. Serena was wearing a pair of red-and-black wool ticked pants and a black sweater the night her husband proposed to her.

The plaids, the velvets, the minks, the leathers, cottons, silks, and denims. If clothes make the man (or woman), then for me, certainly, it's the clothes that make the memory.

I'd love to write a book about all of my Gucci, Dior, and Givenchy outfits and the vintage dress of Princess Grace's that Oleg Cassini gave me for my twenty-fifth birthday. I'd love to tell you the funny story about the time Mr. Valentino came over and we spent an entire rainy Saturday munching on pizza while making up crazy designs for dresses. Unfortunately, none of this has ever happened. Fashionista, I am not. Simply, I am every teenage girl who ever *had* to have the item that all the other girls had, whether it looked good on me or not. I'm the college coed who fell in love with a boy at first glance because his leather jacket made me swoon. I'm the best friend who borrows clothes and never gives them back and the woman who is forty-five minutes late to work because she has nothing to wear. I'm the lover of clothes and shopping whose passionate memories are always connected not only to the clothes that I wore, but what friends and family and boyfriends wore too.

Since I don't have that closet full of all the items that bring back times both magnificent and heartbreaking, these stories are for everyone who keeps an old piece of clothing in the back of the closet, wishing that one day those clothes would get up and start talking about the cherished moments they once shared together.

Learning from the Masters

grew up outside of Philadelphia, but when I look back on my early childhood, it feels to me that I really grew up in the dressing rooms of all the major department stores in and around the city. My earliest memories come from the Lord & Taylor on City Line Avenue. To this day, thinking about the scents of Tea Rose and Chloé perfumes that filled my nose as I walked in makes me wince to the point of nausea. The tiny electric shock I'd get if I touched one of the glass counter displays full of jewelry or handbags should have been a deterrent to turn me off shopping for life. Days at age five and six were spent squirming in a dressing room chair watching my mother, Arlene, and grandmother, Esther, duke it out over whether Esther was a size eight anymore. "It just hugs a little," Esther would say as she blanketed the center buttons of the Geoffrey Beene lilac-colored silk blouse with her uniform gold chains. The eternally size-six Arlene would make a quick switch when Esther wasn't looking and retrieve a size ten.

Later that week, Esther would come over wearing the size eight blouse. We'd know it was the size eight, especially my brother Michael, who'd dive for cover when he realized he was in direct target range. God forbid Esther had opened her arms to hug him; the buttons would have popped out and blinded him.

In those early years, Lord & Taylor outfitted every grand occasion, and I hated every minute of it. It wasn't that I hated the clothes, because in truth, I felt instant adoration. The problem was that I never had a say in my wardrobe. When I was seven, my two shopping superiors ooohed and ahhhed over my first formal dress, a pale blue taffeta ruffley number for my brother David's bar mitzvah. I was strongly against this classic little-girl look and tried to get my way the best way I knew how—by throwing my sixty-pound body to the floor and banging my legs and fists on the ground while shrieking the most deafening high-C shrill imaginable. Seven- and eight-year-old trendsetters in 1977, like myself, favored flowered granny dresses. The particular one I wanted was, in a word, magnificent. Covered in tiny chocolate-and-cream-colored daisies, the dress was fitted with an empire waist and short puffy sleeves. To me, this dress screamed up-to-the-minute, bohemian, "now." The pathetic pale blue abhorrence bawled juvenile, dimestore, Shirley Temple.

"Adena, get up off of that floor right now before I really give you something to scream about," Esther threatened under her breath.

"Come on, Deanie," my mother said, trying to sympathize, "is it really worth all of this?"

"I AM NOT WEARING THAT!" I screamed through my tears.

The purchasing patronizers took a time-out huddle.

"She wants to wear that one," Arlene said, throwing her hands up. "I don't really care anymore. She wins."

"She's going to look ridiculous," Esther countered.

"If she wears that dress, do you really think she's going to ruin the whole night?"

"Yes, yes she will," Esther said, bending down and grabbing one of my arms, as it was in mid-slam. "That's enough with you," she said, pulling me up to my feet.

"Now, look," Esther said, seething as she pinned my arms to my sides, "your mother and I are both wearing blue. You either look like the big ladies, or you look like a bum off the street. I'm going to give you ten seconds to decide."

"BUM OFF THE STREET!" I shouted back in her face.

"WE'RE TAKING THE BLUE ONE!" Esther shouted back.

The fight was over. I was defeated. Esther was bigger than me, stronger than me, her coral ring was digging into my elbow and, truth be told, the thought of wearing the same colors as the big ladies sounded like a really cute idea.

Any lady who lunched always lunched in the Lord & Taylor restaurant, the Birdcage, which in my opinion did not provide an adequate children's menu. Their peanut-butter-and-jelly left nothing to the imagination, except to wonder what cheap company made the runny preserves. I was forced to eat Saltine crackers and drink Shasta soda. Even the décor of the place was uninspiring. Sure, as one might expect, there were birdcages located all around the Birdcage Restaurant. From wire cages to bamboo to plastic, the cages lined the joint. My whole conundrum over the place was simple: Wouldn't anyone in their right mind, especially a seven-year-old, expect there to be actual birds in cages at a place called the Birdcage? There didn't even have to be real birds; they could have had fake birds. But no, the birdcages in the Birdcage held potted ferns.

"It's not about any of that," Esther would explain. "Lunching is to *see and be seen*." And there was plenty of that to keep the place jumping. The problem wasn't getting a table at the Birdcage;

the problem was getting the two *seers* and *be-seeners* to sit down. "Esther!" Aunt Molly Spain, a friend of my grandmother's, would shout out, waving her arm back and forth, and there went Esther. "Arlene, over here!" Aunt Gail Sernoff would call from across the room. Arlene and her Corrèze boots would scurry over to talk to her for at least five minutes, and after that, to Aunt Judy Savitt at the table next to that, and then to Aunt Sissie Lipton, and then Aunt Marjorie Margolies Mezvinsky, and so on . . . and why did I have to call them "Aunt" if they weren't related to us anyway?

"Because they're more than friends; they're family that you got to pick," my mother told me, "and you treat them so for that reason."

"How are you?" I'd watch my mother's mouth as she spoke to the Aunts. "You lost weight," Esther would say, complimenting Aunt Ruth Goldman and Aunt Evelyn Sidewater at the next table.

Twenty minutes later, my scenester foremothers would finally take a seat. That's when the news would come to them. There was a cackle of enjoyment watching Esther's jaw drop in the same swift motion every time news came around concerning the latest "D," which was Arlene and Esther's catchphrase referring to the latest divorce, death, or indictment.

"She turned around for two seconds to go to the refrigerator to get him some margarine and by the time she turned around again he was stone dead, slumped right over the table."

"No!" Arlene had gasped, clutching her chest.

"Yes!" the woman with the lipstick bleeding onto her teeth reported. "Coronary, just like that."

"You have to savor every day," Esther had concluded, bringing her jaw back to its normal position and pinching me under the table until I stopped laughing.

There were, however, good and bad points in going to the Saks Fifth Avenue in Bala Cynwyd, where Arlene got her hair done on Saturday mornings. If you got to the beauty parlor early enough, they had a big plate of soft pretzels next to the coffee. The coiffed ladies would say, "I'll just take a half of one," and then I'd watch them go back for the other half and another half and another half. Some women scooped up a bunch and stuffed them into their purses; that's why you had to get there early.

Saks Fifth Avenue also had a grand staircase leading from the first floor to the second. If one's mother, let's say, was trying on lip liner and was too busy to notice, one might have been able to break away, climb the stairs, hoist oneself onto the broad pine lacquered banister, and slide down to one's heart's content. If, however, in mid-slide, in your eighth year of life, you suddenly realized you had developed a serious case of vertigo, the experience was not as pleasing.

"Just climb back over!" Arlene had insensitively shouted as she went back to testing lip liners. I was, after all, her third and last child. By the time I came around, with two rambunctious older brothers ahead of me, nothing fazed her anymore.

"It's too far, I'm gonna fall!" I screamed, looking down some twenty-five feet below me.

"Wait two seconds and I'll come and get you," she shouted back as she looked at herself in the mirror, comparing shades.

Bonwit Teller on Chestnut Street had the best jewelry sale bin. The game would be to see how many bracelets and necklaces I could get on my body before Arlene noticed. "I can't take you anywhere!" she'd shriek. "Now, take those off!"

Strawbridge & Clothier had a Snoopy Barn, and my Snoopy doll needed a new pilot's jacket so he could face the Red Baron. Arlene felt instead that I needed new undershirts. My mother had insisted she was in too much of a hurry to get into a dressing room, but to this day I'm sure it wouldn't have been such a time-consuming ordeal to walk the two feet into privacy. Instead she insisted, "Oh, come on, no one is even looking" as she took my shirt off in the middle of the children's section and shamed me by exposing my eight-year-old nipples to almost all of the other kids from Belmont Hills Elementary who were shopping with their mothers that day, especially and most regrettably Robby Weinberg, my third-grade crush.

The worst, though, the most wretched and evil of all the department stores in the Philadelphia area that I hated above all, was the John Wanamaker's in Wynnewood. While I disliked the store for its gray walls and lack of pertness in the children's section, it was to become the birthplace of a fear that still affects me to this day.

My mother needed some new pantyhose on our way home from school one day, so she dragged my brother Michael and me into the store with her. By the time my mother got really into the collection of panty hose as she was wont to do, my brother and I eyed our savior from boredom . . . the escalator.

Here was the plan for the big race: Climb the escalators two floors up to the housewares section, do one lap around the Le Creuset pots, touch the blue pot, and head back down to the ground floor. The finish line would be the mannequin of the lady torso wearing the shaper bra. Touch that, and you would be the winner. Since Michael was three years older than me, I would have the advantage. Michael would be climing up the downstairs escalator (the wrong direction) and I would take the upstairs escalator. We would, of course, switch on the way down so that I would again have the advantage.

The 1977 First Annual John Wanamaker escalator competition was on. Michael and I charged up both escalators, and even with my advantage, Michael took the early lead.

"Come on!" Michael shouted to me, slowing down and trying to make the race more even. Michael has always loved competition.

With all the strength I had in my eight-year-old body, before the escalator stair had time to compact under the rubber track, I surged forth. It was then that tragedy struck.

Leaping forward to get off the escalator to the second floor, I was suddenly shot back. The hem of my right bell-bottom jeans leg had lodged itself inside the rubber track, locking me in place and getting even tighter as the escalator continued to roll.

I let out a shrill cry of agony, calling for my brother, who at this point was more than halfway up the down escalator to the third floor.

I could see Michael from the top of the up escalator streaming down to my aid (and, just in case it was a trick on my part, getting to the housewares section and touching the blue Le Creuset pot before coming to my rescue).

By this point, a small crowd had gathered. A security guard tried to stop the escalator to no avail as I screamed on. Michael pulled at my pants to no benefit. My only hope was a superhero of the supreme kind and, luckily, she had finally finished picking out the pantyhose she needed.

"OH FOR CHRIST'S SAKE!" I heard from the crowd, "WHAT HAVE YOU GOTTEN YOURSELVES INTO NOW?"

I cried out in response to that familiar voice and called, "Mommy, Mommy!" As I saw her cross face appear through the crowd, she threw down her John Wanamaker bags, pushed my brother aside, and positioned her arms under my shoulders, yanking me so hard that the bell-bottom jeans slid halfway down to my knees. Then she shook me from side to side until the jeans fell off altogether, leaving me pantsless. Luckily, Robby Weinberg was nowhere in sight. I threw my arms around my mother as the crowd cheered. Just then, the security guard was able to stop the escalator, so she yanked the pants from the conveyor belt, fully intact. Then she looked at my brother and me and shouted, "A MOMENT'S PEACE, THAT'S ALL I'M ASKING! ONE MOMENT!"

For the next few weeks, every time we went to a department store, my mother would stop me before we walked in and say, "Now, look, I need one thing in here. The whole process should take no more than ten minutes; we'll be in and out. If we make it in less, you get ice cream; if you start to cause trouble, I'm going to feed you to the escalator!" I had no choice but to accept the offer.

Without my usual modus operandi to make up for my boredom I began to help my mother pick out clothes and makeup and jewelry. Slowly, I started to enjoy it. She liked it when I told her I hated a particular eye shadow she was trying on, or when I told her she looked like a princess in a sequined Albert Nipon strapless dress. Pretty soon, asking my opinion about clothes was no longer her way of keeping my interest so I wouldn't get into trouble—mine was an opinion that counted. This way of life continues to this day. It was also where an endless bond began.

In the early eighties, while shopping in Bloomingdale's during a day trip to Manhattan, walking over those black-and-white-checked tiles, following my mother back and forth and back and forth, I came across a pair of incredibly cool Fiorucci electric sky blue jeans. They were soooo Debbie Harry, and I was sure if my mom just tried them on, she'd see they'd be soooo Arlene Halpern. My ten-year-old begging pursued throughout the various departments. "I just want to see what they look like," I nagged, and as my pleading began to grind on her nerves, she grabbed the pants from me and threw them over her other tweed and turtleneck possibilities.

Once inside the dressing room, Arlene, who had always gone for Anne Klein classic suit looks rather than Fiorucci trends, grabbed her first item, an Ellen Tracy camel colored skirt that went with a white brocaded top. My anxiousness couldn't take it anymore.

"No, try these first," I said, handing her the jeans.

Begrudgingly, Arlene put her first leg into the pants. It was already clear that they fit like they were made for her. Visions of my mother picking me up from school in front of all the kids in her Fiorucci electric sky blue jeans danced in my head. Everyone would be so jealous that my mom was obviously the chic mom. She watched herself as closely as I did in the mirror as she slipped her other leg into the pants. Maybe she'd even give up the forest green Oldsmobile and get a Datsun 280ZX or a Porsche like Aunt Gail Sernoff had. My mother held in her stomach as she buttoned and zipped up the jeans. There she was: Arlene Rudney Halpern, the with-it, most modish dressed mom in the entire Main Line suburbs of Philadelphia. With those pants, she wouldn't even care anymore when my brothers and I begged for Cheez Doodles and SpaghettiOs. She would be too busy fending off those talent scouts who wanted her to come out to Hollywood and be in a movie with Burt Reynolds or, dare I even dream, be the fourth of Charlie's Angels.

"You know what," she mumbled to herself within the confines of our minute dressing room, "after three kids," she continued, turning to catch a glimpse of her butt, "I could still wear a pair of pants like these."

"YOU HAVE TO GET THEM!" I screamed, causing a woman a few doors down to let out a *"Shhhh,"* as if we were in a library or something.

"Oh, please." Arlene grimaced, unbuttoning my dreams and slipping off our glamorous future. "I'm a doctor's wife."

We left Bloomingdale's that day with my mother's purchase of two turtleneck sweaters and a corduroy blazer. Whether it was my perseverance or Arlene's realization that she had been suffering from an acute case of negative body image, she purchased for herself a pair of Gloria Vanderbilt jeans, much to my euphoric delight.

Two weeks later, Arlene was shopping in a plant store and tripped over a mislaid garden hose. As she fell to the concrete, the force of her fall tore holes in both knees of the jeans. My mother had chipped the bone in her right kneecap and was forced to wear a cast for six weeks. When I saw her throw the ruined jeans into the trash, I feared the worst; there would never be flash in her wardrobe again. The day she got the cast off, however, we went directly to Saks, where she bought a brand-new pair of Calvin Klein jeans. My opinion had counted.

These days, the Los Angeles Barneys department store is my home away from home. I love to arrive at Barney Greengrass, the restaurant inside Barneys, at 1:10 sharp to meet a friend for lunch. One o'clock lunch is the busiest time at Barney Greengrass, and I need to see who's lunching with whom and who's wearing what. That's why I like to get there a fashionable ten minutes late. Dressed in my most au courant (without looking like I mulled over outfits for an hour prior to lunch, of course), I send a kiss over to someone sitting at one table, tell another how fabulous she looks and ask if she's lost weight, and finally sit down at my table, where the gossip comes to me.

After lunch, I consider it exercise when I take the long winding staircase through the floors of the department store. I stop at each department and take a once around: first floor, shoes and accessories; second floor, women's couture; fourth floor, men's ready-to-wear; and so on. Most people eat mashed potatoes or slip on some flannel pajamas to feel those bygone days of childhood comfort. The Los Angeles Barneys is my version of mashed potatoes and meat loaf.

Sometimes I see something that would look perfect for my mother, so I call her back in Philadelphia on my cell phone and describe it to her.

"It's frilly, but it's not. It's simple yet frilly," I tell her.

"It's not too trendy, is it?" she asks.

"Trust me."

"Send it out," she tells me.

My mother and I don't wear the same styles; we don't share the same tastes, but we know which pants or skirt or blouse says "Arlene" or "Adena," or "the new and improved Arlene" or "Adena." It is a language that only she and I can speak, a bond between my mother and grandmother that began many years before I was born, which in turn was passed on to me.

The Devil Wore Treetorns

I have the perfect solution to ending wars: Send the most popular tween girls from middle schools around the world to duke it out. Rather than using guns, explosives, and heavy artillery, all these girls need, these days, is a computer with IM capabilities, a phone, and most important, the must-have fashion item in the must-have color.

Back in my tween days we had the phone, scraps of notebook paper passed around a classroom and, of course, our vicious mouths to torture one another. Although I didn't know it at the time, I now consider myself fortunate to have lived in that era, given the advancements in tween torment technology. We didn't have to have the right Prada bags or Manolo Blahniks that would have forced our parents to take second jobs. In 1981, we had ribbon belts and penny loafers and Levi's and Treetorns with the boomerang logo or Stan Smith Adidas (short for "All Day I Dream About Sex," we'd tease one another) with the black three-stripe accents and shoelaces with blue whales or green frogs printed on them.

I made one of the biggest mistakes of my life in the fall of 1980. I complained to my parents that my feet were in pain. My parents took me to an orthopedic surgeon friend of my dad's who said that I had flat feet, which required a higher arch than my usual sneakers could provide. After the visit to the doctor, and much to my chagrin, my mother bought me deep blue Puma sneakers with a deep yellow swoosh logo. To be honest, I didn't hate the sneakers. I actually thought they were kind of cute. I knew, however, that this was not the right fashion look that was required in the sixth grade at Welsh Valley Middle School. Curses to my feet for not allowing me to wear the white Treetorn tennis sneakers with the boomerang logo like all the other girls had. I had an inkling there would be trouble when I wore the Pumas to school. Had I known the pain I would have gone through as a result of having the wrong sneakers, I would have chosen the foot pain.

"Are they your brother's hand-me-downs or something?" Fern Schwartz, head of the popular girls, asked one day as I gave her an idol-worshipping hello in the hallway.

"They're so retarded-looking," Ali Rose commented.

"I know," I said with a laugh. "They're so ugly, but I have a corrective problem and when my parents took me to the hospital, the doctor said I couldn't wear anything else," I explained, hoping my doctor's excuse would work.

"So you're a retard and you need special shoes," Anna Klem concluded as she laughed with the other girls. "Duh! Everyone knows that!"

This was what I meant in the beginning. Send these girls to Saddam Hussein and Osama bin Laden. Anyone would beg to surrender under this torture.

"LOOK, SHOES ARE SHOES!" My mother had shouted, putting her Stan Smith tennis shoe–clad high-arched foot down when I refused to go to school the next morning. "YOU CAN'T WEAR WHAT ALL THE OTHER GIRLS ARE WEARING! YOU HAVE FLAT FEET! NOW, GET TO SCHOOL!"

"But I can't," I said through real tears. "Fern Schwartz and the other girls said I was retarded because I didn't have the shoes that they did."

"WELL, YOU TELL THEM THAT THEY'RE RETARDED BACK!" My mother was never good with the comebacks.

That afternoon, Ali Rose drew a picture of me and passed it around math class. My blue Pumas in relation to her depiction of my body were four times the size. The caption on the top of the page read I'M RETARDO HALPERN, AND MY DOCTOR SAYS I HAVE TO WEAR THESE GAY SNEAKERS.

If this girl couldn't have taken down Mussolini, I don't know who could.

By Friday night, we got four phony phone calls between the hours of five and seven asking for "Retardo Halpern." At 8 p.m., someone had ten large pizzas sent to my house. I was a mess from the abuse. I sat in my room, crying in fear of what would happen to me on Monday. By Saturday I was comatose.

At about eleven that Saturday morning, I was still in bed in the fetal position, clutching my Snoopy doll with my head under the covers when my father, Barry, knocked on the door.

"Do you want to talk about who you think sent the pizzas?" he asked, taking a seat on my bed.

"No, thank you," I politely declined.

"Mom said some girls were being mean about your sneakers. Do you want to tell me who they were?"

"No, thank you," I politely declined again.

I could sense Barry was at a loss for words.

"Hey," he said with a little more energy as he rubbed my back through the comforter, "your brother and me are going into Ar-den-more to get a new net for the basketball hoop. Wanna come with us?"

"No, thank you," I politely declined again.

"Come on," he said, taking away the covers, "I think you need a present. Isn't there something you want?"

"No, thank you."

"I'm sure there must be something you want," my dad almost begged, "what about that purse that Tracy had? I know you said you liked it. Come on, come with your brother and me."

Truth was, I kind of did want a Bermuda bag like my friend Tracy Soss had, with that cool short wooden handle and inter-changeable purse covers. Tracy went to a different school and told me that everyone at the Shipley School had one. "All you do is unhook these buttons," she'd said, referring to the ones attached to the wooden handles, "and then they have all different colors and patterns that you can get. You can wear a different bag every day." When I asked my mother about it repeatedly, she said, "Maybe," but we never got around to it.

Ardmore, Pennsylvania, is a town outside Philadelphia, which to us suburban Phillites is the shopping mecca of the Main Line. I'd always called it Ar-den-more, which I thought was its actual name rather than the two syllable Ard-more, which became a Halpern in-joke and the only way we've ever referred to it to this day. The shopping areas are divided into two sections, which, when I was a kid, were only allowed to be visited on separate occasions because Lancaster Avenue, the busy thoroughfare that divided the two sections, was too dangerous to be crossed without parental supervision. This actually never made sense, since Lancaster Avenue didn't actually cross the two sections, but we listened anyway. "Up Lancaster" was the phrase used to refer to the upper section, formally called Ardmore West, and the better-suited shopping area for the five dollars your parents gave you to use in the six or so hours they dropped you off.

Everyone from the nerds to the popular kids went Up Lancaster on the weekends, as there was never much to do being a suburban kid. My best childhood friends, not quite the most popular, but certainly not nerds, were Amy Chaikin and Julie Pelagatti. We'd spent countless Saturdays there shopping and flirting with the sixth-grade boys we liked at the time.

The first stop Up Lancaster was what had become the Birdcage of my tween days to see and be seen—the Roy Rogers fast food restaurant, for hamburgers, french fries, and gossip:

"Marci Kleinman went to second with Warren Patruli in the woods behind Mr. Frank's English class," Brooke Lewis whispered to us one day.

"What a slut," we concluded.

Next we'd hit Sam Goody for 78s of Donna Summer's "On the Radio" or Shaun Cassidy's "Da Doo Run Run." Baskin-Robbins 31 Flavors was next door for chocolate-mint ice cream; a hobby shop for a paint-by-numbers set; the leather goods store to buy scrap strips of leather with your initials embossed into them; the MAB paint store to buy white cloth paint hats for twenty-five cents; a Wawa convenience store for Cokes and Cheetos; and our favorite, the Crystal Collage, a gift shop that sold Smurf figurines and pens with fuzzy pink or orange troll-like "hair" and glued-on plastic eyeballs on the tips. Fern Schwartz once told us that we could sit at her table in the cafeteria if we stole a Bonne Bell Lip Smackers from Crystal Collage for her. I was all ready to do it, but Amy Chaikin, forever the one who would never do anything dishonest, was completely against it. Julie Pelagatti couldn't have cared less either way. She was the only tween who didn't care if she was in the popular group or not, a source of strength I have forever admired.

The lower section of Ardmore, Suburban Square as it is called because it's where small boutique clothing shops—including the Strawbridge & Clothier department store—lay in a square surrounding a cement park with tables and benches. Suburban Square was frequented less in those days since we didn't have the know-how or funds to shop there without our parents. It was rare to go to Suburban Square, except if you were going to the Suburban Square movie theater, but that was torn down in the late seventies and made into a farmer's market for vegetables and meats. And what ten- or eleven-year-old wants to spend their five dollars on that? Suburban Square used to make this big deal that it was the "first shopping center in the world," and my brothers and I thought it was really cool because it was in the *Guinness World Records* book. A huge stink was made by some shopping place in Baltimore that *they* were the first, and it turned out that they were right—much to our dismay and sadness.

You never went to Ardmore with your parents on the weekend. If you needed clothes, you went after school on the weekdays. This particular Saturday was an exception, however, since I was so down in the dumps. I called Amy Chaikin, who informed me that Fern Schwartz would not be in Ardmore that Saturday, as she'd heard Fern and the other girls talking in Earth Science that they were going to the Ford dealership where Fern's father worked to test-drive some cars and how cool were they at ten and eleven to be given the keys to brand-new cars? It was a few years before it occurred to me that they were totally lying about that.

So off we went in my father's car, my brother Michael, my dad, and me to Ar-den-more. Although my brother complained, "Why does *she* have to come? I thought she couldn't walk because of her flat feet." My father explained to him that I was going through a very emotional time and it would be good for me. The whole drive over was spent in the backseat with my head hunched over as my dad and Michael sat in the front trying to decipher why the girls in my class sent the pizzas and Michael not being able to understand why we couldn't have kept just one pie.

"They already made 'em," he complained, "what were they going to do with them?"

"I'm sure they get that kind of thing all the time, kids sending pizzas to some poor pathetic kid who's on the outs with the other kids," Barry said.

"Yeah, but we could have shown them that we really wanted the pizzas, and Dean could have gone to school on Monday and told them we really wanted the pizzas and how good they were. Couldn't you, Dean?" he asked, turning to me.

I was out of answers by then.

The funny thing about shopping with my dad and brothers was that they put as much thought into something as useless as a rope-tied basketball net as my mother and I would to ponder over a certain sweater or pair of pants.

"This one's regulated," Michael said, handing it to my father, who compared its strength against another net.

"Yeah, but this one has this rubber coating," my dad said, showing it to Michael, who carefully examined one next to the other. "That should hold better in the wintertime with the snow."

"Yeah, but this one's *regulated*," Michael countered as my father continued to ponder.

An hour later, the assessment was completed and I had fallen asleep on a stepladder in the back of the puzzle and paint section.

"We're ready to go," my dad said, waking me. "Do you want to get that purse you wanted, or should we just go home?"

"No," I said coming to consciousness, "I could go and look at the purse."

Since I had parental supervision, we crossed Lancaster Avenue (or bypassed it, as it were) and went into Suburban Square, where we headed to Strawbridge & Clothier. Into the ladies' purse section we went, which was too much for Michael to handle, so he waited outside in the square, leaving Dad and me to go together. As I went to grab the deep blue one with the light oak handle, a voice from behind called out my name.

"Hey Dean!" I heard as I turned around.

To my delight it was Wendy Mason, who lived down the street from me—a popular eighth-grader whose dad was a golf buddy with my dad and therefore was a friend of mine. She was standing with some other eighth-grade girls, Jen Albert and Nicole Thomas.

"Whatcha doin'?" she asked as I put the purse back on the rack. Remember, I had already made a huge faux pas that week with the sneakers. If a popular eighth-grader like Wendy Mason hated the Bermuda bag, well, I might as well just move out of suburban Philadelphia altogether and change my name.

"Hi Dr. Halpern," she said, giving my dad a hug, which I thought was so cool. She didn't seem as shy in front of my dad as I would have been with anyone else's parents but my own, but I supposed it was because she was a mature eighth-grader.

"Dean wanted to look a these purses," he said, pointing at the rack.

"The Bermuda bag!" Jen Albert shouted. "That's so cool that your dad is getting you a Bermuda bag."

"Yeah," my dad said, proud and excited, "and look, they go with her sneakers!"

The sneakers. In a rare moment of calm, I had forgotten about the deep blue Pumas with the yellow swoosh. Oh God, now the eighth grade was going to be on me about them. And then Wendy, the most popular girl in the eighth grade, said the one thing I needed to hear to end all my troubles.

"Wow, really cool sneaks!" Wendy exclaimed.

There it was, the single defining moment that would end my flat-footed woes. Wendy, head of the eighth-grade gang; stronger, leaner, and faster than Fern and the sixth-grade crew, thought my deep blue Pumas with the yellow swoosh were cool. Life was taking a sharp turn for the better.

"Yes, you should get the deep blue bag," Nicole said. "I'm going to get the pink one. We'll be purse buddies."

Purse buddies with an eighth-grader. I could hear the choir singing *"Hallelujah!"* in my head.

As my dad paid for my purse and Nicole paid for hers, Wendy thought aloud about getting some Pumas in deep blue.

"They're so different from the white ones everyone wears," she said.

"I know," Jen Albert added, "the white ones get dirty so fast."

As we walked out of the store, bags in hand, my dad turned to me and said, "Hey Dean, do you want to stay here and shop with your friends?"

"Yeah," Wendy said, "come with us; my mom will bring you home."

The thought of shopping with the eighth-grade girls was too good to imagine. Why-oh-why was Fern Schwartz at the car dealership test-driving new Fords?

"Go ahead," my dad said, kissing me on the forehead.

It wouldn't be until years later that I found out that my dad had called Wendy's dad for advice about the girls who sent the pizzas. Since Wendy and her posse were going to Suburban

Square anyway, they promised Wendy's dad they'd look for me. Wendy, wherever you are, with all my heart, thank you.

By that Monday, word spread that I was spotted with the eighth-graders in Suburban Square. My Bermuda bag became the must-have item, and since I was the first to have it, it gave me a step up in my popularity. I had taken down Fern Schwartz in a clean swipe and she would never bother me again. I was friends with the eighth-graders and, moreover, Nicole Thomas and I were "purse buddies."

I know my dad didn't realize the grand gesture he'd bestowed on me by having the eighth-graders come to my rescue, but he saved me from an imprisoned life that only tween girls were capable of making worse than purgatory. Thanks, Dad.

I still have flat feet. Given the advancement in shoe technology, though, I can buy any sneaker I want and throw an orthotic in. Who knew that advancements in foot technology could have saved a pizza place from wasting all those extra pizzas?

The Shrinking Dolphin Shorts

The thing about puberty is that it springs up on you so fast, you don't have time to get your bearings straight.

I was in the seventh grade at Welsh Valley Middle School outside of Philadelphia. Fair Isle sweaters with their garland-style necks were the "it" sweaters for 1982. You might as well have just dropped out of school altogether if your polo shirt was sans alligator on your left breast (not to mention the time spent making sure that its soft collar stuck straight up at all times, which was virtually impossible but, nonetheless, give it the old college, er . . . middle-school try). The summer of sixth grade, though, was all about the Dolphin shorts, and since *everyone* who was *anyone* at Welsh Valley Middle had the satin-white-on-the-front, blue-on-the-back short shorts, I had to have them too. Thankfully, my mother obliged and bought me two pairs, which I wore all summer long at Camp Akiba, where the craze had also hit.

Where Julie Pelagatti's boobs became the envy of all the girls and a source of adoration from the boys, I got barely a bump. Where Amy Chaikin's thighs got longer and leaner, mine formed into one uni-thigh. Frankly, by 1982, puberty had turned me into a pimply, no-chest, chubby mess with two sausages for legs.

The first warm day of spring in 1982 meant nothing to me aside from the fact that I had gym class. That morning, instead of packing my sweatpants, I took out the old satin Dolphin shorts that made me feel so chic just a matter of seasons before. We would be running the mile that day, and I knew I had to bring something light to fight the humidity the day had brought.

As the girls in my gym class got ready in the locker room, modestly holding their shirts to their chests so as not to let on what had happened to them that year, I threw on my Dolphin shorts, which I noticed were a little snug, but who cared, and my favorite MY FRIEND WENT TO MIAMI AND ALL I GOT WAS THIS LOUSY T-SHIRT shirt that my friend Tamra Wachs had bought me, and headed out to run that mile.

As I skipped across the indoor basketball court and outside to the track, I felt a strange airy sensation between my legs.

"Oh my God!" Julie Pelagatti shouted as she grabbed me. "Your shorts split," she whispered, "your shorts split!"

Oh my God; my shorts split. The one seam on the shorts, which was sewn right in-between my crotch, had split, leaving me with two patches of satin—a white one in the front and a blue one in the back. Even a slight breeze, or less, an errant sneeze, would blow those two patches right up into the air. What was I going to do? I had missed two gym classes already due to fake illnesses I'd come up with. Mrs. Willard, the gym teacher, had said that if we missed more than three classes, she'd fail us immediately.

I told Julie to go over and ask Mrs. Willard to meet me inside the gym as I kept both sides of my shorts down, being careful not to let my crush, Seth Bonney, know what was going on.

Luckily, everyone in the class was already outside as I waited for Mrs. Willard to meet me inside.

"So what is it, Halpern?" the sporty, lean, and tan Mrs. Willard asked me as she entered.

"Well," I said, showing her as I lifted both sides, "my shorts split."

"Maybe you shouldn't have eaten so much this winter," she said with a laugh.

"Do you think I could skip the mile today?" I asked, suddenly looking at the silver lining. "I don't have anything else to wear."

The burly Mrs. Willard looked down at the clipboard she was holding.

"Halpern," she said, "you've already missed two classes. If you miss this one, I'm going to have to fail you."

So here were my options:

1. Run the mile in a pair of split shorts and suffer the potentially humiliating consequences.

2. Stay back in the seventh grade while everyone else went on to the eighth grade and spend the rest of my natural-born days knowing that my life was a year off kilter because I failed gym in the seventh grade.

3. Sue this fat hater and the Lower Merion School District for millions, get a huge apartment in New York City, and live the rest of my days gloriously and independently wealthy. This was 1982, though, and I was twelve, years before I ever knew that hers was an act of discrimination that could possibly have been punishable by law.

"It looks like a skirt anyway," she said. "Now, come on; we've got a mile to run." She put her arm around my back and led me outside.

"She's making me run," I mouthed to Julie Pelagatti.

Julie crossed herself, kissed her Saint Jude (the patron saint of lost causes) medal, looked at me somberly, and mouthed, *"I'll guard you."*

I situated myself in the center of the pack. My plan was to stay within the confines of the crowd, and that way everyone would be too busy and too close to see my shorts.

As Mrs. Willard screamed "Go," the kids started jogging. I heaved along, trying to make sure I stayed in-between Julie and Amy Chaikin, both of whom had promised to cover my secret. The problem was that the weight I had gained, in addition to the fact that I had not exercised the entire year, left me huffing and puffing so hard, I was finding it next to impossible to keep up with my shields.

Back into the pack I went; everyone was passing me by. Stuart Klempner, who was even fatter than I was, passed me. Steven Harper, who only that morning had gotten the cast taken off his broken leg, passed me. Joyce Sullivan, with her scoliosis back brace strapped onto her body, passed me. I was all alone. That is, until Ritchie Jacobs lapped me altogether, and then Amy Braun, and Lisa Kool. All the while, my split Dolphin shorts were waving in the wind, white satin flapping up in the front, blue satin flapping in the back, MY FRIEND WENT TO MIAMI AND ALL I GOT WAS THIS LOUSY T-SHIRT plastered on my rolls of heft.

I couldn't take it anymore. I was sure I was about to suffer a massive coronary. Oh, the embarrassment my parents would have felt at the funeral from all the whispers! "Such a young girl has a heart attack?" the mourners would ask each other. "What were they feeding her?" I had to stop, just walk a couple of steps; I didn't care if Jeanie Songheart, the class asthmatic, was lapping me as she ran, sucking from her inhaler.

Soon enough, I was in dead last. Half the class had already finished, and I still had two laps to go.

"What's with her shorts?" Ritchie Jacobs screamed as I neared the bend in front of the resting class.

"What's going on there?" Sarah Miles shouted. "Hey, she split her shorts!"

Pretty soon the whole class, including Seth Bonney, who I now knew for certain would not be asking me to Spring Dance, pointed and laughed as my Carter's underwear exposed themselves to everyone.

"Come on, Halpern," Mrs. Willard shouted. "Just pack it in; you're finished," she said both literally and figuratively.

I walked off the track, gasping for air as Julie and Amy came to my aid. They said nothing as they rubbed my back and uttered sounds of teenage angst and distaste.

That day at lunch, word spread fast that my shorts had split. Some versions acknowledged my white Carter's underwear. Another version had me not wearing any underwear at all. Somehow, I just had to let the whole thing roll over me, but it took years for that to happen.

The following week on gym day, it was one hundred degrees in the shade. I wore my brother Michael's red sweats, which were three sizes too big.

I got a C− in gym that year, which suited me fine, since the following year Mr. Lowell, the eighth-grade girls' soccer coach, had an affair with Kara Ellison, a ninth-grader, and my split Dolphin shorts became a distant memory.

It Was His

I've always been envious of my girlfriends who grew up with sisters. Both Julie Pelagatti and Amy Chaikin had sisters, which afforded them double the wardrobe. I was not as fortunate. I had two athletic older brothers who could not have been less concerned with the clothes on their bodies. A shirt was a shirt to be worn, even if it had holes in it or hadn't been washed in weeks.

"I don't know which one's worse!" Laner, our housekeeper and second mother, shouted to them as she surveyed both their rooms blanketed in clothing and other debris. "You boys wanna be the death of me?" They ignored her as they did their daily situps. "Because I'll tell you something. I'll walk right out of this house right now and never come back before that happens! Now, clean up these rooms before I set you both over my lap and beat you till I see the whites of your eyes!"

The thought of Elaine "Laner" Womble—all 4'11" and ninety pounds of her on a good day—throwing my varsity-wrestler brothers over her lap and beating them senseless always made for a good laugh. The thing was, whether it was the threat in Laner's words or the respect she commanded, the boys inevitably picked up a couple of shirts and threw them in a drawer or emptied a trash bucket. Their efforts usually made no difference, but to Laner, it was the principle.

"That should teach them a thing or two," she grumbled under her breath as she nodded to herself in satisfaction.

It was the truth, though. For my brothers, David and Michael, their worlds were not about fashion or cleanliness or respectfulness. In David's senior and Michael's freshman year at Harriton High School, the boys wrestled at 105 and 126 pounds, respectively. Since I was the chubby little sister, and basically weighed the same as my oldest brother, David, even though he was seven years older than me, I was elected his grappling partner for training purposes. David had spit, sweat, and exercised relentlessly to get down to his weight while I ate Jiffy Pop popcorn, french fries with cheese, and Ring Dings to reach mine. No sooner than I would say "Please don't hurt me," David would have already grabbed me in a half nelson, flipped me and my red Sassoon jeans over his shoulder, and thrown me onto the wrestling mat set up in our basement, his elbow knifelike in my chest. No matter how much I screamed in pain, he'd want to try it again as Michael stood along the side of the mat, coaching him.

"This time, throw her a little higher before you drop her on the ground," Michael instructed. "It knocks the wind out of the opponent."

This was their world. There were no girlfriends, just other pimple-face boys who raided our refrigerator. These boys had odors as bad as "the funk of forty thieves," Laner would say. I never heard gossip about the high school kids, except once when some guy got kicked off the wrestling team for rigging the scale so he would make his weight for a match. Dirt, grime, and the ever-present sound of a football, basketball, or baseball game blaring on some television heavily overshadowed any feminine customs in my house. Therefore, if Laner had actually left like she kept threatening to, I would have never been taught her three most important rules to living a ladylike life:

1. "Always have lipstick on when you leave the house, because you never know when some nice-looking man is gonna want to sweep you off your feet."

2. "Jergens Hand Cream. You can try all the expensive ones you want, but I'm telling you, Jergens is the only one that's gonna keep your hands soft."

3. And most important to her—why, I still don't know, though I always take it into account if the situation ever presents itself—"Dean," she'd say and smile, "always love a man in a Cadillac. A man in a Cadillac will always treat you right."

After David graduated from high school, he moved into an apartment in downtown Philadelphia with his best friend Rob Meyers and started his college career at Temple University. For as much of a slob and violent offender around the house as he was, I missed my big brother and instinctively continued to tiptoe when I walked by his room at two o'clock on a Saturday afternoon when he would usually still be sleeping. I began to long for that jackass who'd bang on the bathroom door for me to "hurry up" and "don't use all the hot water," the entire time it took me to take a shower. Michael was gone for the most part too. Since he and David were perpetually joined at the hip, he was always staying downtown at David's apartment. At that point, since both my parents worked, it was just Laner and me after school watching her soap operas, or "stories" as she called them, on television. I would eat a Ring Ding or two before she slapped my hand, warning me of my ever-increasing weight gain.

In the early part of David's sophomore year at college, he met his first girlfriend, much to my chagrin.

I took an immediate dislike to Debbie Penderstein and her slender frame, long brown hair, and immaculate clothing choices. So did Laner. "Who does she think she is, coming in here with her bony behind and designer clothes, leaving her plate just sitting there on the table and not bringing it to the sink?"

Debbie really did have the most beautiful taste in clothes, though. Her blue-and-white-striped sailor top and matching white wide-leg pants with matching blue lace-up Espadrilles left me salivating. The black Chinese Laundry sandals she wore with black pants and a Fair Isle sweater made me jealous beyond words. She always smelled like lilacs and she never had a hair out of place. Frankly, David and Debbie looked like Beauty and the Dirty Beast. What she with her elegant, French-tip nails saw in my long-haired, ripped-jeans, and permanently-stained-sweater brother was beyond my grasp, but David was in love.

"Hey, *Bubbah*," David said calling me by the nickname I'd asked him repeatedly not to call me, "look at how pretty Debbie is." He kissed her on the cheek.

For as much as I didn't like Debbie, she didn't like me much either.

"Hello, Adena," she'd snarl at me as she entered our family room where I was watching television. "David and I want to watch a movie. Do you think you could go someplace else?"

We had absolutely no reason to dislike each other; it was one of those things. My brother Michael even told me that Debbie said

I was on her "blacklist." And even though I had no idea what a "blacklist" was, she was on mine too.

On the first night of Hanukkah, my mother decided to have a family dinner in the dining room—something we never did. We were never a very religious family, even for a gift-giving holiday like this one. Debbie always had this sort of one-upmanship attitude, and I think my mother felt it too, so that's why she did it. I was against this Hanukkah dinner from the start, but was promised Laner's famous lasagna in return for my suffering.

As we lit the candles on the menorah (no prayer was said since no one knew one), gifts were handed out. Debbie got me a purple address book with little flowers on it.

"Aw. That was so sweet of Debbie to get something for little *Chunk-a*," David said. He kissed Debbie on the cheek while I asked him yet again not to refer to me by yet another disparaging nickname.

I was told that I got Debbie a scarf, which my parents picked up and signed my name on the card, which she seemed to dislike immediately upon opening the gift. Good. We were even.

She handed David her gift to him, which was packaged in a shirt box from Boyd's in downtown Philadelphia. Boyd's is a very expensive men's store that I had only been to once when I stopped off with my dad when he had to pick up a new tuxedo shirt and cummerbund for a party he and my mother had to go to. Everyone knew, though, that Boyd's was the pinnacle of men's fashions in Philadelphia, so whatever was in that box, it had to be of the best quality and, thus, a waste, given my brother's tendency to be so indifferent when it came to clothing.

I grabbed another chocolate-chip cookie from the tray and began to go at it, ignoring my parents' fawning over the gift that hadn't even been opened yet. I heard the sound of ruffling tissue, followed by my mother saying, "Oh, Debbie, that is gorgeous!" What I heard next were trumpets of exultation blaring in my head as I turned for a second and caught my first glimpse of the splendor coming out of that box.

It was truly the most beautiful sweater vest I'd ever seen. Chocolate brown in color, the sweater had three large argyle diamonds going down the front in pastel pink, blue, and green.

"It's really nice," David said, kissing Debbie on the cheek.

Nice wasn't even the half of it. It was *so* my brother David to simply disregard a sweater as beautiful as that. One thing was for sure, he would never wear it. Another thing was for sure, I would.

As I awoke early the next morning for school, there was one thing on my mind: that gorgeous sweater vest. I jumped out of bed and ran downstairs to the last place I'd seen it—the dining room, where of course it was still sitting. I pulled it out of its Boyd's box and took it upstairs to my room, where I matched it with a pink oxford underneath and my Sassoon blue jeans that were so tight, I had to lie flat on my bed and pull my stomach in, in order to button them. I had never looked more fashionable or more beautiful in my whole entire life.

I went to school that day and struck a pose everywhere I went.

"Cool sweater!" Mrs. Langoustine, the cooking teacher, said.

"Where did you get that?" Amy Chaikin asked the minute she saw me.

I could have had a theme song for me as I walked through the halls that day. I was like the cover of a beauty magazine, and the sweater was giving me the confidence to prove it. Even as the bus let me off down the street from my house, my neighbor Peter Sernoff, who never spoke to me since he got into the popular group said, "That sweater is really nice, Dean."

I strolled into the house that afternoon and walked up the stairs, shifting my hips from extreme left to extreme right as I entered the kitchen to find Laner sitting at the kitchen table. She looked exhausted and heartbroken, like someone had died.

"Dean," she said softly, "what went on here today, I don't know how I lived through it. Your brother is so mad at you, and I'll tell you something, I don't blame him. How could you take his present that Debbie got him and then go off to school in it?"

Had she hallucinated?

"Because he never would have worn it. You know that!" I told her. "He even left it here!"

"He left it here by accident, and then he purposely came back to get it this morning to wear it out to lunch with Debbie's parents. Jesus wept. When he looked in that box and realized that you'd taken it, I thought he was spent to go out of his mind!"

I knew she was telling the truth, as I could almost hear the echoes of his rant. The cause to create drama and shrill, deafening tantrums by any of the five Halperns was a standard custom in our house.

"He started going on and on. 'How could she do that?' And then Debbie started putting her two cents in, 'That sister of yours is a spoiled brat who has to get everything she wants!' Don't you worry. I told that Debbie to mind herself when she was talking about one of my kids, but Dean, you didn't think he'd wear it and I never thought he would have worn it, but how could you just take it without asking?"

She had answered her own question. Who would have thought he would wear it? No one. It was a given, and yet still, I felt worse than awful.

"Dean, you take that sweater off and fold it up nicely and put it back in that box, and I don't want to ever see you do anything like that again, you hear?"

I took off the sweater and neatly folded it like she told me. A couple of hours later, I was in my room with the door shut when

I heard David and Debbie come into the house. No one knocked on my door.

For the next three years that David and Debbie dated, David's wardrobe got better and better—a sweater with no holes, a pair of pants that hadn't frayed—and I never borrowed a thing, not even that really cool jean jacket with the Michael Jackson-esque sideways zipper pockets and fringe coming off the sleeves that David only wore once. No one ever mentioned what I did. I didn't exactly get punished for it, but my remorse stayed longer than it should have.

A couple of years later, when I was fifteen years old and my parents went away for the weekend, I decided to invite some kids from school over—which turned into the entire school, complete with beer kegs and cigarette burns on my mother's good couches. It was getting way out of hand, but I was too afraid to do anything about it. I couldn't call my parents or my brothers, because they would have gotten mad at me for inviting people over in the first place. As I was looking through my old purple address book with the little flowers on it, I came across Debbie's number. She was living downtown and didn't have a car to come and help me, but offered to stay on the phone with me until things calmed down. I went up to my parents' room and shut the door and for the next four hours, Debbie and I talked about everything from where she got her clothes to the fact that we both thought Andrew Ridgley from Wham! was super hot. It was the first time we ever really had a conversation, and although it wasn't exactly what was said between us that was important, we were finding out we weren't the enemies we thought we should be. A few weeks after that, David and Debbie were going to see a movie and asked if I wanted to join them. The delight in my face said it all. Somewhere around my Sweet Sixteen party, Debbie and David broke up and I was truly sad about it. I still think of her from time to time and hope she's well and as fashionably dressed as she always used to be.

Years after the breakup, I was hanging out with Laner in the laundry room, as I was wont to do as she folded some clothes that David had dropped off. I saw her take the sweater, mangled and pilled, out of the washing machine. "Why I'm doing this, I don't know," she said as she placed the seriously decomposed sweater vest on a hanger to air-dry. The sweater had been worn and torn to tatters, but he was still wearing it. Whether it was the memory of his first love, or the fact that he had nothing else to wear and didn't care, I'd never ask him. David was never the type to divulge girly things like that.

"Hey, Sugar?" Laner said with a laugh, "you think he'd be mad if you wanted to borrow this now?"

A Shorts Story

Remember when young women started doubling men's boxer shorts for actual shorts? You saw sorority girls wearing them with sayings printed on them stating something like GAMMA GIRLS KICK BUTT!

Well, guess what. I started that.

Thank you. No applause, please.

I really did, though. You can ask Amy Chaikin or Julie Pelagatti. Ask my parents; they'll tell you, "Oh yes, she started that. She was at the fashion forefront on that craze."

I don't know what gave me the idea to go into my father's drawers drawer and cop a pair of his boxer shorts. He really couldn't understand it either.

"What's the matter with her?" my father asked my mother. "She keeps taking my underwear. That's not normal."

"She's a teenager," my mother declared. "I used to wear poodles on my skirts when I was her age."

"You can't compare poodle skirts to a fourteen-year-old girl taking her father's underwear," he complained.

I wore them anyway—not to school or anything, maybe to the Wawa convenience store for more Ring Dings, but that's about it. Since they were a little big in the waist, I folded the fabric over and fastened it with a safety pin, thus covering up the front hole pocket—a double bonus. It looked ridiculous, but man it was comfortable, and it hid all my bad parts, which at that time I thought were many.

"Dave and Lou saw Adena in Wawa wearing my underwear," my father complained to my mother. "I get patient referrals from those guys. She is not to wear my underwear anymore. I don't understand it, Arlene. We buy that girl all these nice clothes—I see the credit card bills—and she insists on wearing my underwear!"

"It's a phase," my mother told him. "She just got her period and she doesn't like the way she looks. I wore my cashmere sweaters a size too big."

"You can't compare cashmere sweaters to wearing my underwear! This has got to stop! ADENA!" he screamed to me from the kitchen.

I was in the family room in his boxer shorts and an extra large T-shirt eating some Jiffy Pop popcorn and watching *Knots Landing*.

"What?" I griped with a mouth full of corn.

"Get into the kitchen. Now!" he yelled.

I slumped in, bowl of popcorn in hand.

"I'm only going to say this once," he said, giving me his angry, two-fingered point. When my father pointed at you with both his index and middle finger, you knew he was serious. "Fourteen-year-old girls are not supposed to wear their fathers' underwear. I work day and night so you have all those nice clothes in that closet of yours. I see you wear my underwear again, and you're going to be punished."

Can you imagine?

"Are you coming to the party this weekend?" a friend would ask. "Can't," I'd have to tell them, "I'm grounded for wearing my father's underwear."

So I bought my own boxer shorts, same brand as my dad's—Hanes—in his size.

"Whose are they?" my dad asked as I walked by, chomping on a Ring Ding.

"They're mine," I muttered through the chocolate cake and whipped cream center in true teen-angst form as I went into my room and shut the door.

It was around that time that I had my first major crush. Stanley Denton didn't go to my school; he went to Lower Merion High School. I'd seen him playing at a Harriton vs. Lower Merion soccer game. Soccer was to my neighborhood what I'm assuming football is to other parts of the country. It was the sport to play, and it made celebrities out of the guys who were on the team. You'd get dressed in your best relaxed Levi's and Koala Blue or ACA Joe sweatshirts that you'd cut the neck wider on so it would slide off your shoulders like Jennifer Beals in *Flashdance*, then you'd sit in the stands and watch the most popular and cutest Harriton boys like Eddie Blume and Robert Weiss kick that ball back and forth from one end of the field to the other, scoring goals, and pretend each point was in your honor.

Julie Pelagatti was dating one of the players on our team, thus giving Amy and me the slick VIP groupie status of getting to go onto the field after the game to congratulate our players. While Julie made out with her boyfriend, Amy and I took the opportunity to scope out some of the other guys up close. Stanley Denton was talking to Robert Weiss, and I went over to say congratulations. As Robert introduced us, I fell into teenage lust. Stanley was sweaty and dirty and wearing the wrong team colors, but his light brown hair was shabby and long, covering his eyes, and he had the coolest gold stud in his ear.

"Hey," he said.

"Hey," I said back.

It was love. I stood there thinking of romantic ideas as I hunched my shoulders in the hope that the side of the ACA Joe sweatshirt would fall over my shoulder.

I couldn't ask Robert Weiss for the setup; we didn't have that kind of friendship. Just then, Debbie Ellick and Lori Levin walked up to Stanley and interrupted our deep conversation and, although I walked away, I found my in. I knew that Debbie and Lori were friends with my friend Jennifer Klein, who went to the Friends Central School. If Debbie and Lori were friends with Stanley, then it was a good chance that Jennifer was too.

"Of course I'm good friends with Stanley," Jennifer declared on the phone later that night when I got home. "I was just at Lloyd Bucher's keg party with him last Saturday night! Why? Do you like him?"

"I think he's cute."

"Do you want me to say something?"

"If you want."

The setup was put into motion. How amazing was it going to be: me, dating a soccer player. Granted, from a rival school, but who cared? I would be a traitor for the man I loved. How romantic.

A couple of days later, I was in my house after school watching *General Hospital* in the family room. I was sitting there with a box of Ritz crackers and a jar of peanut butter, dipping my finger into the jar and spreading the contents onto my cracker when the doorbell rang.

In retrospect, I should have asked who it was at the door. In retrospect, I should have been doing my Jane Fonda Workout tape instead of eating butter crackers and peanut butter in the middle of the afternoon. In retrospect, I should have been doing a lot of other things, but most of all, in retrospect, I should not have been wearing boxer shorts that were three sizes too big with the Betsey Johnson multicolored neon-orange, pink, and lime patchwork cropped sweater I'd worn to school that day when I opened the door to try to lure Stanley Denton into my life.

"Did we catch you at a bad time?" Jennifer asked as I stood in the doorway with peanut-butter-soiled fingers.

"No," I hastily replied, "come on in." In retrospect, I should have said, "Yes," and slammed the door on them.

"This is Stan," Jennifer announced as they walked in.

"Hey," I said.

"Hey," he said staring down at my shorts.

We walked back into the family room, and I sat there as composed as I possibly could, sneaking licks of my fingers to get the peanut butter out of my fingernails. I sat on the edge of the couch, crossing my legs and sitting up as straight as I could. Stanley was even more gorgeous clean than he was on the soccer field. He had these piercing blue eyes that could have been mistaken for being colored contacts. I got the chance to get a peek every time he moved the hair out of his eyes.

"Crackers?" I offered, handing him the box.

"Got a game in a little," he said, looking over at the television watching Luke Spencer duke it out with one of the Cassadines. "Actually," he said, looking over at Jennifer, "we really can't stay long."

My heart dropped.

"We just came over to say hi," Jennifer said. "We were passing your house, so I thought we'd stop," she lied.

Two minutes later, they were gone. An hour later, Jennifer called me.

"Were you wearing your father's underwear?" she screamed into the phone.

"No, it's my own," I told her.

"Why were you wearing boxer shorts? He thought you were a weirdo!"

"Well, why did you come over without calling first?"

"Because I didn't expect you to be wearing your father's underwear!"

"What did he say?"

"He said, 'She's a chubby weirdo!' Who wears their father's underwear?"

Teenage girls can be so vicious with the truth, can't they? Jennifer, though, was one of my best friends, and for that reason had a right to tell me the truth. In return, a couple of years later, I told *her* the truth when she asked me what I really thought of her nose job.

"He's actually dating Robin Zinman," she lied.

"OK," I told her nonchalantly.

"Sorry," she said.

"Oh, I don't care," I told her as I hung up the phone.

I threw off the boxer shorts and put on some regular shorts, then shoved the Jane Fonda Workout tape into the VCR.

A few weeks later, Laner confused my boxer shorts with my dad's boxer shorts and put them in his drawer. When I saw my dad wearing my underwear, I didn't bother saying anything. I could have teased him and said, "What father wears his daughter's underwear?" But he wouldn't have thought that was funny. I would never wear boxer shorts again, even when the craze hit the sorority circuit across America. It was like Einstein regretting having helped invent the atomic bomb.

Every now and then as the years go by, I'll be out with my parents at the beach or on a hot summer day, and lo and behold, there's some girl wearing a GAMMA GIRLS KICK BUTT! pair of boxer shorts. I'm telling you now, I could win the Nobel Peace Prize and when reporters ask my parents how they feel, I'll bet you anything they'll say, "We're proud about this, but did you know that our daughter was the first young girl to wear boxer shorts?"

"Look, Dean. She's wearing boxer shorts, and you started that!" my mother will shout with glee, pointing at the college coed.

"That's right, you did," my dad will proudly say. "Remember how she used to steal my underwear, Arlene?"

"I sure do," Arlene will say boastfully.

"Who knew she was such a trendsetter?" my father will announce.

I want to tell them both to shut up, but I really don't have the right. I mean, let's face the facts: I *did* start the trend. Proud as they could be, smiles bright and fulfilled, my parents will stand there and watch in awe at the contribution their daughter added to this world until the sorority girl has turned a corner and left their sight.

"Who knew?" my dad will say with a sigh.

"It's really something," my mother will agree.

Years later, I did eventually end up dating Stanley Denton.

"Why were you wearing your father's underwear?" he teased.

"Teenage angst," I told him.

Oh, How I Wannabe You

As the start of the tenth grade rolled around, my body had started to "wean out the baby fat," as my mother put it. I was sitting at home watching MTV in my fifteenth year of life when a woman came on the screen who changed my outlook on fashion forever.

Teased blond hair wrapped in what seemed to be the bottom ribbing of the half sweatshirt she was wearing. Long pearls snapped against her shiny BOY TOY belt buckle as she shimmied back and forth. She wore a short black crinoline skirt over a pair of biking shorts and black boots. In short, she was awe-inspiring, and the whole thing was giving me the shivers. In the two minutes that I watched the video, she spoke to me as being exactly who I wanted to be. She was cutting edge, sexy, playful, feminine yet one of the guys, tough, independent, and radical all rolled into one. I had to look exactly like her. I needed to be her twin, and thank my lucky star, I kind of looked like her already . . . at least I thought so. When I asked Amy Chaikin about this possible switched-at-birth phenomenon, she said as tenderly as she could, "Well, you both have blond hair."

The most important thing was this: I had to get this look down before anyone else found out about her. Chances were, no other girl at school would have seen the magnificence like I did. No one in suburban Philadelphia had the keen fashion eye that I did and could pick up on this singer's obvious up-to-the-minute air of aptness. As I stood in front of the bathroom mirror showering half a bottle of my mother's VO5 hairspray onto my head and teasing the matted locks with my brother's comb, I thought to myself, *If anyone accuses me of copying, I'll deny it to the end.*

"You look like that singer on MTV!" Greg Garron shouted the second I walked into homeroom that Monday morning.

"What are you talking about?" I asked with the straightest look I could manage as I nervously scratched my face. I immediately regretted it since I might have smudged the fake mole I'd created from mascara that morning.

"You do! You do! You look like Madonna!" Debbie Franklin joined in.

"Who is Madonna?" I asked nervously as I fiddled with the silver bracelets I'd spent all Sunday night creating out of some silver wire from the hardware store.

"That singer," Debbie said, "on MTV."

"I don't have MTV," I lied as I ran my hands through my teased coif and straightened the do-rag tied around it.

As I sat in my seat and listened to that morning's roll call, I could feel the eyes of my peers upon me like vultures circling my combination chair/desk, getting ready to attack at any moment. How could they have all found out about her in one weekend?

"Adena Halpern?" Ms. Greaser, the homeroom teacher, asked taking roll call.

"You mean Madena?" Greg Garron snickered.

The crowd went into hysterics. I was mortified.

I went into the bathroom before first period and wiped the faux mole off my face. Maybe it was a little too much.

It was my first lesson in perpetrating a look: Never go for the entire look head-on, just go for little nuances of it.

The next day I arrived in class, my hair was still disheveled, since that was the part I liked the best, but I eighty-sixed the mole, the wire bracelets (which were poking into my skin anyway and I was afraid they would slit my wrists), and I wore a pair of Girbaud neon-orange parachute pants with my blue-and-white-striped Vans sneakers. I knew I looked like the bastard child of Madonna and Bozo the Clown, but I was my own person, not a carbon copy of someone else.

I've seen Madonna through almost every stage of her material life. When Madonna cut the do-rag and went like a virgin, I was enthralled. Not only was I like a virgin, I *was* a virgin, and the bustier I found at Screaming Mimi's gave me the figure that would soon make me otherwise. When she affixed a long faux ponytail and played Truth or Dare, I took the dare and sadly got that ponytail stuck in some subway doors. The last I saw of my faux mane, it was kind of waving good-bye as it flapped in the wind when the subway took off and made its way toward Grand Central Station.

I did skip the geisha look, and when Madonna came out with the sex book, I skipped that look too.

These days, Madonna has been more apt to wear tailored suits, which really aren't my thing, so I've sort of broken off from her, but I'm always on the lookout for her new styles. Just last week I saw this paparazzi photo of her coming off a plane in a multicolored orange, green, and yellow three-quarter-sleeve sweater matched with an orange scarf. I've been looking everywhere, but I can't seem to find anything that looks remotely like it. If you see something like it, could you call me?

Madonna is, was, and will always be the queen bee to my wannabe.

The Impossible Dream

knew exactly what I wanted to wear for my senior prom, and nothing was going to stop me. What I wanted was very simple: a black strapless top with a knee-length crinoline poufy bottom. In the late eighties, with Madonna and Cyndi Lauper as our teenage fashion idols, how hard was that going to be to find?

Amy Chaikin already had her prom dress: a feminine white strapless, tight-lace, floor-length gown that she'd matched with some white gloves and a white sash she'd tied around her neck. When I started on the quest with Julie Pelagatti, the first dress she tried on was the one she got: a gold lamé strapless that sprouted hoards of stiff fabric in shades of gold and white on the bottom of the floor-length gown, making her look like a gold mermaid. Personally, I didn't like the dress, but conceeded the point when Julie said, "I want my prom dress to reflect who I was in my senior year of high school." Looking back, both dresses reflected who my friends were at the time. For Amy it was her ethereal nature, always looking on the bright side of everything. For Julie, her dress was a shining example of someone who was nothing like everyone else and did not care what anyone else thought. I, on the other hand, wanted to look like everyone else, but with a bit of myself thrown in for good measure. That's why I thought my idea of the black strapless with the crinoline was perfect.

With my two best friends set and ready to go, I still had my own dream to conquer. I searched everywhere, all the department stores in my neighborhood, except of course John Wanamaker's, which I hated and was positive they wouldn't have had anything cool in there anyway. I checked all the boutiques in downtown Philadelphia. Zilch. I went to visit my brother Michael at college in Washington, D.C. Zip. My cousin Michele and I took a day trip to New York City. Not even close.

Was I asking for such an impossible notion? All I wanted was a simple black strapless dress with a knee-length crinoline bottom! They had gold mermaid dresses out there, but God forbid a simple black strapless with a knee-length crinoline bottom!

"Look, I know you've got your heart set on one thing," my mother announced one day as I got home from school, "but I found a backup just in case."

"Oh, Dean," Laner said, "you are going to love it!"

Like a curtain unveiling a priceless work of art, Arlene slowly hiked the Saks Fifth Avenue chocolate-brown plastic covering over the hanger of the dress to reveal a Victor Costa blue-and-white polka-dot strapless tea-length dress with a blue-and-white ribbon tied around the bodice. My mom and I were big Victor Costa fans; he was a designer for the masses who knocked off some of the hottest dresses around. When Ivana Trump, a personal icon of Arlene's, announced that she in fact wore Victor Costa dresses on occasion, Arlene knew she had concrete evidence that he was one of the most important designers (or redesigners, as it were) of the time.

"I couldn't resist," she said, taking it off the hanger and placing it against my body. "If you don't like it, Gladys at Saks (Arlene's favorite saleslady of the time) said we could return it."

I put the dress on and modeled in front of the mirror.

"It's stunning," my mom gasped.

"Princess Diana, look out!" Laner cried out.

I liked it; I kind of really, really liked it.

"You don't like it," my mother sighed.

"She hates it," Laner sighed.

"No, I like it," I sighed.

"But you have a dream," my mom said, frowning at Laner, who in turn threw her arms in the air in exasperation at me.

The dress went back into the chocolate-brown plastic wrap curtain and stayed in my mother's closet for a week until she finally took it back to Gladys at Saks, much to the chagrin of Gladys, who was sure the next time she saw it, I would have been wearing it in my prom picture.

"She has a dream," my mother said, handing the dress to the dejected Gladys who, in turn, handed my mother a return slip.

After two months, with the exception of—blech—John Wanamaker's, I had exhausted my search through the entire East Coast of the United States of America. I was done.

I gathered my mother, Laner, Amy Chaikin, and Julie Pelagatti, those closest to me who had tried their best in helping me see the dream come alive.

"Ladies," I said taking a deep breath, "I regret to announce that I will not be attending Harriton High School's 1987 senior class prom due to the fact that I have nothing to wear."

Some were not strong enough to take the news.

"OH, FOR CHRISSAKES! SHE'S GONE OFF HER ROCKER!" my mother shouted, storming out of the room.

I looked at those who had the strength to stay, sighed, and picked up the phone to call my date and tell him.

"What if you *made* the dress?" Laner wondered aloud.

I put the phone down, smacked my head and yelled, "Eureka!" I was going to make the dress! How hard could it be?

"Mom!" I screamed, "I'm going to make the dress!"

"I'm calling Gladys to save the Victor Costa just in case," she shouted from the other room.

"FORGET IT!" I screamed back at her. "I AM NOT WEARING THAT STUPID BLUE POLKA-DOT THING!"

"YOU'LL BE SORRY!" she screamed back.

"I HAVE A DREAM!" I shouted in teenage defiance.

"FINE! GO LIVE YOUR DREAM!" she shouted back, and then into the phone, "HEY, GLADYS? FORGET I CALLED! MY DAUGHTER IS A LUNATIC!" Then she hung up.

I didn't speak to my mother for the rest of the day.

For the next week, Amy, Julie, and I combed the stores, trying to find the right parts for my dress. Again, there was trouble. We found the crinoline, but the crinoline was see-through, so we bought two and figured we'd put one over the other. When Laner saw that it was still see-through, she went out and bought me a black slip to go underneath. I had the bottom taken care of.

It was becoming a bit more difficult to find the top, though, and the search was wearing on my army.

"I have finals to study for," Amy said when I asked her to come with me to Delaware for the day.

"I'm looking for some gold hoop earrings to go with my dress," Julie said.

"Wax buildup," Laner said, pointing at the pristine floor.

I knew I had reached madness, but I was determined that if I never saw my classmates again, the last time they'd ever see me, they'd see the prettiest, most fashionable, and original-looking girl at the prom. I was *this* close, and even though all of my supporters had fallen by the wayside, I was still marching on.

I decided to head to South Street, a place I had already checked, but figured it was worth one more go.

South Street in Philadelphia was, in the late eighties, the shopping zenith for up-to-date funky duds. If they didn't have what I needed, then I was done. There was one place I hadn't tried on South Street—a thrift store whose name I forget. The store isn't there anymore, but I'm sure you could figure out where it was. The joint smelled so bad, demolition couldn't have fumigated it.

South Street might have been funky, but this thrift store *smelled* too funky. The stench of mothballs, combined with a particular armpit fume meant I had only a short amount of time before I'd start to gag, so I sucked in my breath and searched quickly. As luck would have it, the third dress I saw had the exact top I had envisioned—a velvet bodice that curved around the boob area, which could give my flat chest area a nice line. It was a little damaged and worn-looking, but I was at my wits' end. I didn't even bother to try it on and quickly paid the three dollars for the dress, declining a bag and leaving with the dress in hand. Driving home, I had to stop at the dry cleaner's and leave it there to be deodorized. When I arrived at my house, I passed my mom on the way up the stairs.

"Found the top portion," I bragged.

"And the dream deepens into reality," she said with a wince.

Two days later I got the dress back, clean and de-fumed. With one day left before the prom, I had no time to think of anything else.

With scissors in hand I went thread by thread as I detached the bodice portion in order to fasten it to my crinolines. An hour later, I was ready. It was then that it occurred to me: The bodice had a grooved edge and the crinolines had an elastic waist. I had no idea how to sew it, and we didn't own a sewing machine, but I was committed to seeing this through. Visions of Molly Ringwald putting together her prom dress in *Pretty in Pink*, a film I'd seen the year before, danced through my head. I worked through the night, meticulously sewing each strand as delicately as I could. By 4:00 a.m., my eyes started to give out, so I drank a six-pack of Coke to see me through. By 5:30 a.m., prom day, I was finished.

As hard as I'd tried, my sewing was not perfect. In fact, it was dreadful. When I put the finished dress on a hanger to get a better look at the whole creation, my heart dropped. The dress was awful. It looked like a third-grader sewed the thing together, as jagged lines of thread zigzagged through the middle of the dress. The bodice was too old and shabby-looking, and the crinolines weren't as poufy as I wished they would have been, but there was nothing I could do about it. I could never tell anyone how I really felt. I had no one to blame but myself, so I'd have to lie and act like I thought it was the prettiest dress I'd ever seen, even prettier than that Victor Costa blue-and-white polka-dot number. I tried to convince myself that maybe I could construe it as being punk-looking, but it was a stretch, even for the punk look. I had been so dramatic about the whole thing, had made such a big deal over it. I felt like I had failed. I had no choice but to put on a brave face and go with it.

Laner, my mother, Amy, Julie, and I convened in my bedroom as I unveiled my creation.

Silence filled the room. I caught my mother glancing at the jagged threads. Laner had this frozen blank smile on her face. Her mouth was agape.

"You know what?" my mother said, "it's actually adorable. I'm very proud."

"It's just beautiful, Dean, good for you," Laner said, kissing me on the cheek.

"It's really pretty," Amy said.

"It's something you'll never forget," Julie said, and smiled.

Were they lying? Sure they were, but even to this day they would never tell me otherwise.

As we entered the room, the ethereal white, gold mermaid, and black pouf promgoers surveyed the other dresses. One dress caught my eye. I took a closer look. . . . Melanie Kaplan was wearing exactly what I wanted! Where did she find it? China?

I walked up to her and smiled as our crinoline poufs brushed up against each other.

"Love your dress," I said, smiling.

"Your dress is really cool," she replied with a polite grimace.

"Yeah, I made it," I tried to say proudly.

"I got mine at John Wanamaker's," she said as my world collapsed.

As we grooved through the night, I tried not to think about my dress and began to truly enjoy myself, dancing with my friends and celebrating this last hurrah. By the end of the evening, some of the stitching had come undone, leaving a gaping hole on the side of the dress. By that time, I was done with the whole thing anyway.

A year later, during winter break from my freshman year of college, I went with my parents to see *Broadcast News*. When the movie got to the scene where Holly Hunter gets dressed to go to the Correspondents' Dinner with William Hurt, my mother and I started screaming so loud; we could not believe our eyes. Some of those in the theater told us to shut up, and if we could have stopped the movie for a second and explained our outburst, we would have. Holly Hunter was wearing the blue-and-white polka-dot Victor Costa dress.

For those who have asked me through the years what I wore to my prom, after reading this story, you're probably a little perplexed. Yes, I lied, and I apologize. I did not wear the Victor Costa blue-and-white polka-dot dress like I told you, the same one that Holly Hunter wore in *Broadcast News*. Now you know what I really wore.

The Beautiful Boy in
the 8-Ball Jacket

first laid eyes on Adam in September of my freshman year of
college, 1987. I was late in meeting a new friend for dinner and
as I approached her dorm, I rushed up the stairs and into the
lobby. As I followed a fellow student through the locked doors
that led to the dorms, a voice from behind stopped me.

"Excuse me," I heard as I froze, letting the door lock in front
of me, "do you have ID to get into this building?"

"What?" I said, turning around and nervously fluffing my
teased and Stiff Stuff–sprayed coif, "I'm here to see . . ." (whatever
her name was; I can't remember).

"Good for you," he answered sarcastically, "but I'll need to see
some ID if you think you're going anywhere."

I knew that I had forgotten my ID, but I looked through my
canvas army surplus that doubled as a purse with REM and U2
pins on it as if maybe my ID wasn't still on my dresser where I
remembered leaving it. I had taken the wrong subway and crossed

twelve blocks to get to my new friend's dorm, and this guy was going to make me go back and get it?

"I forgot it at my dorm," I told him, hoping for sympathy.

"What's your name?" he asked.

"Adena Halpern."

"Where do you live?"

"Hayden."

"What floor?"

"Third."

"Well, I'm just going to have to pay you a visit sometime to make sure you really live there." He smiled shyly as he winked.

My jaw went slack as he came into focus.

He was, in a word, gorgeous. Tall though, taller than I had ever been attracted to before, and he had this flawless olive complexion with these amazingly thick, dark, curly locks hanging in front of his brown eyes.

"So you don't really work the desk?"

"Nope," he said. "I'm just an innocent bystander, trying to make sure this dorm is safe." He smiled as he unlocked the door to let me in. I smiled back as I walked through the door, and watched him as it separated us.

"See you around, Miss Halpern," the beautiful, taller-than-I'd-ever-dated boy said as he continued to smile and walk away. As he turned to walk out of the building, my heart swooned. On the back of his red-white-and-black-patched leather jacket, a huge circled 8, like a pool-table 8-ball, was emblazoned. It was meant to be. Eight was my lucky number.

I ran up the stairs to my friend's dorm room.

"OK," I screamed, out of breath, "I totally just met my new boyfriend!"

"Who was it?" she asked.

"Tall guy. Dark. He had a big eight on the back of his jacket."

Her face soured.

"Adam?"

"Is that his name?"

"No way. You do not want to go out with him. He's bad news."

"Why?" I said as my heart began to hurt.

"He's just . . . he's such a *poser*! He walks around with that 8-ball jacket like he owns New York. He thinks he's so cool!"

That was the end of my friendship with her.

Adam got my number from student services and called me the very next day. We set a date for coffee the following afternoon.

As was the case so many times in my many short years of life, I had nothing to wear. If Adam was cool enough to wear that 8-ball jacket, there were cooler things to come. I looked into my closet. No to the Levi's with the hole in the butt; no to the stirrup leggings; and definitely no to the Girbaud white parachute pants when I tried them on. My roommate said I looked like the Pillsbury Doughboy in them.

I decided on a black-and-white-checked poufy skirt, which hit just above the knee. I had gotten it at my favorite store, Mooshka, in Philadelphia before I left for school. I matched it with an Esprit cotton off-the-shoulder black top, because I always thought I had sexy shoulders. I teased my hair as high as it would go, gelled it with Tenex, sprayed it with Stiff Stuff, and put on my Janet "Miss Jackson if you're nasty" immensely huge hoop earrings that I had looped my parents' house key on, and was set to go.

As I opened the door to my dorm room to greet him, the eighties were over.

Except for the 8-ball and red-and-white patches, he was head-to-toe black. Cool black: black jeans, black T-shirt, black shoes. I was Cindy Lauper who had stuck her finger in an electric socket. He was even taller and leaner and more muscular than I remembered him being, and I immediately regretted wearing my Chinese silk slipper flats.

Standing in front of me was the epitome of sleek and with-it, and I felt like I looked like yesterday's decade.

As we walked outside, Adam reached into his pocket and pulled out a pair of black Ray-Ban sunglasses. He talked all the way down Third Avenue, but I couldn't hear what he was saying. All I could think of was how amazing he looked in those sunglasses, all the while worrying that some passerby smoking a cigarette might get too close to me and set my hair on fire from the inestimable amount of flammable product I'd put in it. The sun was beating into my eyes, my legs were glowing they were so white, pebbles were lodging themselves inside my slippers, and I only really came to consciousness when Adam stopped me and put his hands on my shoulders. "Can I just say"—he smiled sweetly—"you have the most amazing eyes."

By the following week, the Tenex was thrown out, the Stiff Stuff bottle was being used as a doorstop in my dorm hallway, and heading down University Place were two slick lovers in Ray-Ban sunglasses and black leather jackets—his with a circled 8-ball emblazoned on the back—holding hands. The five-foot-tall girl had on black leggings, a black T-shirt, and her blond hair was sleek and straight. The six-foot-two-inch, taller-than-tall, olive-skinned boy wore his Levi's with his wallet attached to a silver chain hanging out of his pocket. As he scooped her up in his arms and kissed her, she was sure that they were the snappiest dressed, most in-love couple that New York City had ever seen.

My Life in Six-Inch Heels

The greatest thing about Adam was that he never noticed my obvious foibles. He never commented on my practically transparent pale skin, or the year I had to spend growing out my damaged split ends from all the teasing and hair spray. He never mentioned that I had a couple of pounds to lose, but he did grab my waist when I finally did lose those pounds and said, "I have to watch out for the other guys because my girlfriend is getting sexier looking every day." All of those things, however, were a distant second to what really bothered me and what didn't faze him.

It was not uncommon for some jerk-off, sometimes drunk, though most times sober, to come up to us and ask, "How do you two have sex if she's so short and you're so tall?" Even though Adam always gave the same answer, "Very well, thank you," it still bothered me to no end. I'd raise my voice at Adam afterward and say, "Why didn't you belt the guy?" Adam would say, "What do I care what he thinks?" The problem was, I cared. Adam was a foot

67

and two inches taller than me. As much as it bothered me, it was what it was and there was nothing I could do about it but try to make up for my height with my one-and-a-half-inch cowboy boots and forget about it. Still, whenever the subject would come up, like when the ubiquitous schmuck would approach us, it was something that truly irked me.

In the spring of 1990, my junior and Adam's senior year of college, we had just left a matinee showing of *Jules et Jim* at the Bleecker Street Cinema. Adam was a film student who had dreams of moving to Hollywood and becoming the next Martin Scorsese, and I was his faithful girl who loved the movies as much as he did. As we threw on our requisite shades and leather jackets (the 8-ball jacket by this point had been put in the closet for posterity and had been replaced with a motorcycle jacket; I wore a simple one with black buttons) we decided to walk into SoHo for shopping and coffee.

We drifted into a shoe store, and Adam tried on size-thirteen black Doc Martens and I glanced over to the women's rack. Perched in the middle of motorcycle boots and Converse All-Stars was a particular shoe that caught my eye. It was a pair of six-inch platform sandals to be exact: black, faux suede, size five—my size. I took off my one-and-a-half-inch-heeled black cowboy boots and slipped into the six-inch platform sandals. Suddenly I was up with the rest of the world. The air seemed clearer. I had to put on my Ray-Bans because the light seemed brighter.

"What do you think of these?" Adam asked. I looked down at his shoes and then up to his face. It was incredible. The strain in my neck was gone.

"Your shoes are really cool," I said. "What do you think of these?"

He looked down at my sandals and then into my eyes.

"They make you look tall," he said.

"We'll take both pairs," I said to the saleswoman.

For the next week, the only time I took those sandals off was to go to sleep. I had gone from the middle of Adam's chest to almost close to his shoulder. We could practically dance cheek-to-cheek, and I didn't have to stand on a chair to do it. The best part, though, was what I thought of as I threw my arm over Adam's shoulder as we walked into Nell's nightclub that night: Since my pants were long enough to go over the shoes, no drunken putz in a dark bar would ever know the difference.

After two months, Adam threw away his Doc Martens because they were giving him blisters. I wore those sandals, even in the winter with snow on the ground, for the next three years. I'd had the soles re-stitched four times before they died a horrific death involving a tree stump during a hike in the Santa Monica mountains.

These days, I don't care what anyone else thinks about my shoes. I don't feel comfortable unless I'm in a heel that could give me a nosebleed from the altitude. My brother calls them "stilts." Random people come up to me on the street and ask me how I can walk in them. I've had my boots called "a KISS reunion." If friends mention me in conversation and the other person is cloudy as to who I am, my friend will say, "She always wears high heels," and the person will remember.

On a shoe hunt, if a salesperson asks if they can help me, I always say the same thing: "Show me your highest heel." Ninety-eight percent of the time, the heels aren't high enough, so I'm left with a surprisingly pitiful number of shoes in my closet for a Jewish princess with a shopping addiction.

Now that I've been walking in heels for so long, I have trouble walking in flats. Last September, my neighbors were having their living room painted and I went over to spy. I had just come from the gym, the only place I'll be seen in flats. While doing my best impression of Gladys Kravitz from *Bewitched* I tripped over one of their steps in the front yard and fractured my metatarsal bone in two places. I had to wear a cast for six weeks. When my neighbors came out to help me, one of them said, "She's in sneakers, too. This girl really can't survive without those heels."

Was it Adam's taller-than-tall height that caused me to desire a more elevated existence? No. It was, however, the final straw. Truthfully, I can't remember a time in my life when I didn't hate my height. At my high school graduation, out of three hundred kids, I was the first to graduate in my class because they lined us up by size. The laughs that came from the crowd when the principal asked for the shortest first. . . . I still have nightmares. I had been called the dreaded "Teenie Weenie Deanie" way too many times to mention. By the time I finished college, I was sure that I had spent more money on alterations than I did on my tuition.

I fear the day I have to go to a foot doctor and he tells me I can't wear high heels anymore. I will never stand again. I'll be one of those divas who lounges in bed all day, and friends and fans can all come to me. I'll have to buy pink boas to wear over my nightgowns and turn my bedroom into a lair of lust with peacock feathers and satin. If I have to go to the bathroom or run to the fridge, I'll wait until everyone leaves. Then again, I'd miss too many great parties. Maybe I can persuade Mr. Louboutin to make orthopedic heels.

Los Angeles–Just One Look

I n the summer of 1991, I graduated from college and moved to L.A. to be with my college sweetheart. Since Adam was a year ahead of me in school, he had already moved a year before. I did not want to move to Los Angeles. I had come to love New York and all the fashions it had to offer. Although I had visited Adam a few times during the year, fashion had not been on my mind. He was. At that point in my life, if Adam had wanted me to join him in the Hare Krishnas, I would have found a way to work with my bald head and toga.

I really loved my style in the early nineties. I was really into tight-as-could-be Levi's paired with Lycra ballet tops that fit my twenty-year-old (never-been-to-a-gym-and-didn't-need-it-and-should-have-relished-the-experience-more) body, and of course, my six-inch platform sandals. I had become a hip chick. SoHo and any piece of clothing it sold was my utopian paradise.

As I headed out of the airport terminal to wait for Adam, I

took out the small wire-rim Ray-Ban sunglasses he'd asked me to pick up for him that he couldn't find in Los Angeles. As cool as we were in New York, we'd be cooler in L.A.

When I saw Adam drive up to the terminal and get out of his beat-up Volvo, a voice I'd never heard before popped into my head.

"Go back into the airport, get back on the plane, and go back to New York," the voice inside me said as my taller-than-tall boyfriend in the yellow-and-orange-flowered Hawaiian shirt grabbed me and kissed me.

"Tell him it's for your own good, and go back into the airport and go right back to New York," the voice said again as I ran my fingers through the greasy gunk that compressed his luscious locks of dark curls.

"Your hair," I said, wiping the grime off my hand and onto his Hawaiian shirt. "What's with your hair?"

"You like it?" he said, smoothing it back. "It's the look here."

"Go back into the airport! Just say you made a mistake and go back!" the voice shouted in my head.

"It's OK, I guess," I said with a face that told him just the opposite.

"It's different here because of the weather," he said, taking my suitcase and throwing it into the trunk. "It's nothing like New York."

As we drove back to the apartment we'd now call ours, the voice inside me had calmed down long enough for me to hear Adam say, "So guess what? How would you like to go to a movie premiere tonight? My boss gave me his tickets."

A movie premiere? I suddenly loved Los Angeles. My next thought, what to wear, was immediately followed by the voice in my head starting to rant again.

"Can it!" I told the voice.

This was 1991, a few years before E! Entertainment Network,

so the closest I got to seeing a movie premiere was either seeing it on *Entertainment Tonight* or watching the old clips of stars like Lana Turner and Frank Sinatra get out of long limousines and adjust their fox stoles and tuxedo jackets.

"I don't think I have anything to wear," I told him.

"You just wear whatever," he said, "This is L.A. It's all about the comfort and none of that New York *posing*."

"So I can just wear jeans?" I asked him, thinking that I could pair it with a black ballet top.

"Well, something a little nicer than that."

Adam had to go back to the big director's office to finish the day, and as he dropped me off, he said, "I'll drop you off at the Beverly Center if you want to find something new. You'll take a cab home."

So I did.

As I strolled the faux marble floors of the Beverly Center mall, I noticed a very strange phenomenon. Every store had the exact same look. Cheap Lycra flowered dresses—granted, in different colors and different types of flowers—were displayed in shop windows. I thought they were all horrible. I hadn't worn a flowered dress . . . well, ever. In 1991, Los Angeles had nothing. No story, one look. There were very few Los Angeles designers, there was no Bloomingdale's or Barneys like there are now. New York designers didn't have stores there yet. There was Neiman Marcus and Fred Segal, but I couldn't even afford to walk into those places. Maybe I was getting ahead of myself though. Maybe Lycra flower dresses were where fashion was going. After all, Adam had informed me a week before of all the firsts that Los Angeles created: "Barbecue chicken pizza, aerobics, EST, and the space shuttle." Maybe they were on to something with these flowered dresses.

"This is what I was talking about," the voice said. *"For your own good, go back to the airport!"*

I dispelled the voice and tried on a Betsey Johnson turquoise floral print. It wasn't me, but obviously neither were my first inclinations of living in Los Angeles. I decided to give it a try and live the West Coast way.

That was until I realized I'd left my wallet at home.

I walked the three miles home in defeat. When I finally got back to our apartment, the left shoe of my six-inch platform was pus-soaked from the blister that had formed and popped on my big toe. I ransacked my suitcase for any kind of clue as to what to put on, and settled on a pair of black leggings with a black suede button-down vest over it. To me, it said chic. It might not have been the floral look, but screw 'em all. I was from New York . . . by way of Philadelphia.

If you've never been to a movie premiere that you have absolutely nothing to do with and you don't know anyone else there, I'm telling you now: It sucks. Yes, you get all the free popcorn and all the soda your teeth could ever want to decay for, but truthfully, you will never hear a more silent sound than when you walk down the red carpet with your taller-than-tall olive-skinned boyfriend in matching wire-rim Ray-Ban sunglasses and absolutely no one wants anything to do with you. The spotlight goes out, the sounds of the clicking cameras stop. You almost think you see the throngs of photographers and reporters look at you, then look at one another and say, "They're no one. Let's go get a cup of coffee."

Still, Adam and I walked down the red carpet hand in hand with our heads held higher than high, me in my black on black, he in khakis and a Hawaiian shirt—this time with pictures of tropical settings and pineapples with the words OAHU and HONOLULU and KAUAI captioning the locales. Maybe they didn't know us now, but how could they know if the picture may have been worth millions someday?

As we entered the theater and took our assigned seats next to

Sylvester Stallone and his then-girlfriend, now wife, Jennifer Flavin, I knew there was a reason I had forgotten my wallet. Jennifer Flavin was wearing my almost-bought turquoise flowered dress, and since I was sitting right next to her, the effect could have been devastating for both of us. I looked out into the crowd and saw an ocean of flowers and Lycra. I felt like Rudolph Valentino's Lady in Black, but I really didn't care. I was it. They were not. Screw the voice in my head. I was staying, and if for no other reason than to give Los Angeles one more look.

It Just Doesn't Go

Five years later, there was not a stitch of cool in Adam's closet. He had adapted to the relaxed linen styles of Hollywood as I pored through the Sunday *New York Times* Style section, trying desperately to conform to what people living three thousand miles away were wearing.

"Hi, Nancy," he'd say, wincing at my black miniskirt, leather boots, and too much liquid eyeliner. "How's Sid?"

"I don't know," I'd retort, staring down at his white patent-leather Gucci loafers. "Maybe he's stuck in the seventies at the country club, ordering a highball. You'll tell him hello when you see him."

You had never seen a couple who had come to look more diametrically opposed. That divergence escalated into an unending series of arguments that only later did I come to discover resulted from our agitation in trying to lead each other in two separate directions we were unwilling to explore together. At least that's what the shrink said.

"It's old-school, baby," he explained in a ridiculous Rat Pack impersonation one day when he met me wearing a mint green linen suit he'd matched with a mint green tie.

"It's grunge," I shot back as he stuck his finger in the hole I'd created on the side of my thrift-store sweater.

We had grown up together, but had fashionably grown apart. While I wouldn't go as far as to say that it was his white Gucci loafers or my all-black attire on a ninety-degree day that put the final nail in the coffin of our relationship, I will honestly say it was a part of it.

"That's your boyfriend?" my boss asked me after meeting Adam, who'd worn gold cuff links to my office Christmas party. "I thought he was your tax attorney."

"Sorry about your girlfriend's leg problem," a coworker of Adam's whispered to him in his office one day. "Does she wear those platform shoes because one leg is shorter than the other?"

I've always thought of dating as being like your credit record: After a few years, the bad parts just don't count anymore. It's been years since I said good-bye to the romance I'd come to know with my first love. It's been years since the sadness and bereavement of breaking up pitted my heart. Life went on. I choose not to remember the bad parts of our relationship because what's the point? So I just don't. All that's left in me are those isolated memories of two young people who loved each other very much. I'm envious of that seventeen-year-old girl with the Ray-Ban sunglasses who felt so safe and free to express her devotion. I feel so sad for that twenty-six-year-old woman in perpetual mourning attire who realized that nothing in life is guaranteed.

It had to end. So we said good-bye. I would never know him as an ex-boyfriend. He would always be my college sweetheart.

We might not have been willing to head in the same direction anymore, but he would always have a place in my heart for one simple reason.

Nine years earlier, Adam, the taller-than-tall olive-skinned boy in the 8-ball jacket, had not only changed my attitude on style, but taught me a lesson that as much as I try to have faith in, I never really believe. I've seen it time and time again in the romances of my friends, my family, but I never trust that it will happen again in my own life. So sometimes at night when I'm sad over my latest breakup, I say these words that I try to accept as truth, and hope that they will finally sink in: It will never matter what I'm wearing, or how I think I look. There is always the possibility of a beautiful boy who can see right through it.

The Vera

Right after Adam and I broke up, instead of taking that trip to Europe to drown my sorrows in a glass of Venice or Paris, I went to Barneys and impulsively purchased a $4,000 Vera Wang black gown. It's a fabulous frock, yet very simple. It has a sheath front and a cowl drape in back, with a band of mesh fabric around the small of the back for the surprise of seduction.

Everyone said I'd gone off my rocker. No one applauded my purchase. "Nuts," they'd said behind my back. "The chick needs to be admitted."

I had no special occasions coming up when I bought the dress. The whole thing about it was that I knew I wasn't buying the dress to wear it in public. I bought it for those sad nights. It was a (and I even fully admit, a very ridiculously expensive) symbol that the best was yet to come. Whenever I got very depressed, which in the beginning was a lot, I'd put on the dress, a hot pair of stilettos, some makeup, and frolic around my apartment until I felt better. I'd talk on the phone, watch television, accept pizzas from the delivery guy, play video games on my computer, pay my bills, and do my laundry, all in my Vera Wang gown. I think I logged a year's worth of wear in the dress in the confines of my apartment until, slowly, I didn't need it anymore.

One day I was sifting through my closet, throwing out old clothes, when I came across the Vera. I had no need to put it on. My source of depression had been gone for the past five years. It was time to move on.

I took the Vera over to a resale shop and put it on consignment. They offered $750 for the dress, and they'd keep half. Sure, it was highway robbery for a dress that took me two years to pay off, but $325 was fine enough for a dress I was never going to wear again.

That night the chest pains started.

It was like leaving a puppy on the side of the road. Something that had made me so delighted at times, something that had touched my soul in the deepest part of my darkest, bleakest time, and I was giving it up for $325. Money was not the issue when I bought it, why should money have been an issue when I parted with it?

The next afternoon on my lunch break, I ran back to the shop to reclaim my Vera.

I entered the store and proceeded to present my case.

"I've made a grave mistake," I said in distress. "I want my dress back."

The saleswoman looked at me cockeyed.

"Which dress was it?"

"The Vera!" I exclaimed.

"That black dress?"

"Yes, the black gown with a sheath front and a cowl drape in back, with a band of mesh fabric around the small of the back for the surprise of seduction."

"Oh, we just sold that," she said with a laugh. "That's so weird. Here's your check."

Dejected, I left the store with my check and headed over to Baskin-Robbins thinking that I'd drown my sorrows in a $325 vat of chocolate mint.

I headed into the ice-cream store behind four teenage girls, who were holding up the line talking.

"He's gonna love that see-through part in the back," one girl said to another.

"I know. I can't believe I scored a Vera Wang at that store!"

"Hold it," I said. "Did you just buy my Vera Wang gown at that consignment store?"

"Who wants to know?" the tough one of the group asked.

"The one whose dress it is. And I'll give you all your money back."

"No way," the new owner said. "That's my prom dress. You go get a new dress."

"But that's my breakup dress. I need it."

The girl looked at me cockeyed. I suddenly felt ridiculous.

"Oh forget it," I said. "Enjoy."

And as I got my ice cream, I passed the girls on the way out.

"Hey, what's a breakup dress?" my purchaser asked.

And so I sat with them and explained what the dress had been to me.

"Jeez, that was dumb," the tough one of the group said. "Why didn't you spend that money and go to, like, Paris or something?"

Maybe it was dumb and maybe it wasn't. Still, it's nice to know that my dress went on to make someone else happy.

And maybe next time around, I'll buy a Vera Wang gown for a much better reason . . . hopefully in white.

The Fake Prada

had bought this great Prada knockoff bag on a weekend trip to New York City for $40. Please don't tell the government. It's a black quilted tote with a magnetic button closure and a zippered pocket in the lining. When I got back to Los Angeles, bag in hand, I got more compliments on it than I could count. Even the salesladies at Barneys couldn't tell the difference.

"That is a great bag," one of them said to me.

I wore that bag for about a year. The triangle Prada emblem on the front slipped off at one point, so I Krazy-Glued it back on. It never came off again.

One day at about four in the afternoon, I was driving to the Pavilions supermarket in West Hollywood on Santa Monica Boulevard. It was a hot sunny day and my air conditioner wasn't working, so I had to put down all the windows so as not to suffer a heat stroke. If you're familiar with Santa Monica Boulevard in West Hollywood, you know that this is a very busy thoroughfare.

Patrons sit outside at streetside cafés; lots of people are always on the sidewalks—something not too common in L.A. That's why what happened is so odd.

There was a red light at Santa Monica and Robertson Boulevards, so I stopped, being the honest motorist I've always been. I had my head in the clouds. I don't remember what I was thinking about—most likely my shopping list.

The next thing I knew, a young man—Caucasian, late twenties/early thirties, reddish-brown curly hair, and wearing a somewhat-yellowed white T-shirt with green ribbing on the neck and sleeves—stuck his hand into my car and snatched my fake Prada tote, which was sitting on the passenger seat. It only took seconds for the assailant to commit the horrific offense, but to me it all happened in slow motion, and I can still remember the thief's face to this day. You don't forget the face of a mugger who steals a highly authentic-looking quilted Prada tote that even the salesladies at Barneys can't tell from the real thing.

I didn't scream. I was actually surprisingly calm about the whole thing. There was traffic behind me and, truthfully, you don't want to piss off L.A. motorists in traffic. I just know that the person in the car in back of me clearly saw the crime being committed, but did they stop and ask if I was OK? Did they honk their horn? No. That's L.A. traffic for you. Your fake Prada tote gets stolen right out of your passenger seat? Your tough luck; move it along. I watched the villain run off behind some stores and into an alley as I calmly put on my left turn signal and made a U-turn toward the West Hollywood Sheriff's Department, which is ironically located a block from where the vicious felony occurred.

I walked in and approached the desk.

"A bandit stole my Prada bag out of my car," I told the female officer.

"Was it real?" she asked me.

"Practically!" I told her. "It was a really good fake," I said, speaking in a language only women can understand. "Even the saleswomen at Barneys couldn't tell the difference."

"You know that fraudulent designer bags are also an offense," she answered, making me feel like a cheap pariah.

"Yes, I'm aware of that," I acknowledged, when I really wanted to say, "But all the other girls have them too."

She had me fill out a police report, and that was that.

I went home, canceled all my credit cards, grabbed some loose change I had lying around, and went to McDonald's, where I treated myself to a super-size order of fries. Given the tragedy of what had happened, it was only right.

I was really sad about that bag. It was such a good fake, and I felt really ritzy carrying it around every day. I mean, I didn't cry about it or anything, but I was a tad emotionally stricken.

Two days later, I got a call from the West Hollywood Sheriff's Department. They had found my bag. Can you imagine? The thief had cleaned me out of the $40 and change in my wallet and had thrown the bag in an alley. My credit cards and driver's license were still in the bag. I don't know who found the bag—no one said—but I thank you, wherever you are today.

I still have the bag, though I don't use it anymore. Although, come to think of it, maybe I will.

The moral of the story? Don't leave your purse on the passenger seat on a hot day when you have to put all the windows down? I still do, though. Get your air conditioner checked before those hot summer months? Must get to that. The real moral of the story? Don't cut the tag inside the fake purse that says MADE IN TAIWAN. Not even the most heinous of pinchers will want it.

The End of the Line

As I headed into my late twenties/early thirties, I didn't have anything left that didn't come from me and only me. I paid my own bills, so if I went over my credit limit, I had no one to turn to. It was all me and, at that point, after paying my own way through life for the past (give or take) ten years, it gave me a nice Mary Richards "You're gonna make it after all" buzz. At twenty-seven, however, there was one teensy-weensy little part of my life that I just couldn't let go of.

Just before I'd left for college years before, my mother gave me a Bloomingdale's card and a Macy's card.

"It's just for emergencies," she had said at the time.

To most parents, emergencies consisted of being locked out of your dorm in the middle of a snowstorm or to pay a ransom in case I was abducted.

Here was the kind of emergency she was talking about: "I found a dress for the formal. I'm just sitting here watching *The*

Today Show, and they're having a spring fashion show. I just saw the cutest pink strapless and it's exactly what you need. I called Bloomingdale's. They have it in your size. Use the emergency card."

I know. My parents are fantastic.

OK, so ten years later, with a job of my own, a growing savings account, and no mortgage or car payments to worry about, I still had those cards. While I cannot say that I didn't use them, it was a very rare day when I did. The fact remained, I could not survive without them, and it came down to a simple little fact: Those cards were my only remains of a wonderfully spoiled Jewish princesshood. They were simply a reminder of a time gone by. If all else failed in my life, Mommy and Daddy were there for me in the forms of Macy's and Bloomingdale's credit cards. To have those cards taken away from me, even if I never used them again, would have destroyed me. Three thousand miles away from my family and no boyfriend anymore, it would have said to me that I was truly alone in this world. There was no one who loved me but me.

As I said, I have a wonderful relationship with my parents. Arlene and I truly are the best of friends. Every now and then, however, Arlene gets in a bad mood and needs for someone to feel worse than she does. Since I am her best friend, I am usually that person. One particular night, however, she went for the jugular.

"And another thing," she said in the middle of our phone conversation. "I saw that you bought some mascara on the Bloomingdale's card last month. Don't you think it's time you started paying for your own mascara? I want those cards back already."

"Please, Mommy," I begged, "don't take away the cards, I won't use them anymore."

"So what's the point of having them? I want those cards back. It's time for you to be on your own."

"Please just let me keep them."

"Fine. We'll compromise. Give me *one* of the cards."

Suddenly I was Meryl Streep in *Sophie's Choice*.

"Take the Macy's, take the Macy's! . . . No, wait!"

I tried to compare the pros and cons of each store.

Bloomingdale's had the better clothes.

Macy's had the better bedding department.

Bloomingdale's gave out food samples.

Macy's had my favorite Lancôme saleslady.

"Did you hear me?" she asked.

Macy's had a great parade.

"Why are you being so quiet? I'm giving you one more minute to decide."

"Can I sleep on it and get back to you in the morning?"

"NO! PICK ONE!"

"I DON'T KNOW!"

"TIME'S UP! I'M CALLING AND CANCELING THE BLOOMINGDALE'S!"

"STOP SCREAMING AT ME!"

"YOU STOP SCREAMING AT ME!"

"YOU'RE SCREAMING AT ME!"

"I'M HANGING UP AND CALLING!"

"MOTHER, IF YOU'D GIVE ME ONE MINUTE WHEN YOU WEREN'T SCREAMING, MAYBE I COULD FIGURE THIS OUT!"

"TEN SECONDS. Ten, nine, eight, seven . . ."

They just kept swirling through my mind. Macy's . . . Bloomingdale's . . . Bloomingdale's . . . Macy's . . . oh God, the horror of it all.

And then the most wonderful thing happened.

"WHAT'S ALL THE SCREAMING ABOUT?" I heard as my dad picked up the phone.

Arlene explained the whole thing to him.

"Christ, Arlene, she doesn't spend anything! She's all alone in the world, let her keep the goddamn cards," he said.

I heard the phone slam. Arlene fell silent.

"Fine, he's right." she said.

"Thanks, Mom."

"OK, I love you."

"I love you too."

And so I was left with both cards intact, but because of what had taken place, I sent her the cards the very next morning. That conversation showed me something that I had totally forgotten, a simple fact that had completely slipped my mind: No matter how old I get, no matter the financial status, I will always, without a shadow of a doubt, be Daddy's Little Girl.

The Five Women You Meet in Los Angeles

The neatest thing about living in Los Angeles is that everyone, for the most part, is from someplace else. No one has family here unless they've formed it on their own. It's like *Lord of the Flies* with grown-ups. When I moved to Los Angeles in 1991, besides Adam, I knew absolutely no one. All that was to change very quickly, however, when I met the five women who, fifteen years later, are still my closest girlfriends. When I look back on those early days, I can only picture my five compatriots in those cheap Lycra flower dresses that we all hated, but because it was L.A. style at the time, and we wanted to be a part of L.A., we wore them anyway. Luckily, fashions got better and, over time, those dresses became the symbol of what brought us all together in the first place.

One of my inconsequential late-twenties/early-thirties birthdays in the late nineties was all about celebrating estrogen-style. I felt like going expensive and decadent, so we decided on Spago.

My friends arrived at the restaurant in the same order as they entered in my life.

Susan was first. She'd actually told me she might be late, but knowing her as well as I do, I knew she'd be the first. My friend Susan is the busiest person I know, and yet she always makes it on time. That's one of the things I love most about her. I'm all about punctuality and so is she. The thing is, I don't have a tenth of what her schedule is, so this lady gets extra stars in my book. Susan is one of those women who, in my opinion, "has it all." After working her way up the Hollywood corporate ladder and becoming a top executive in a leading television company, while in the meantime also getting married and having three kids (two are twins no less, and I had to kid her, "You always have to do things the hard way, don't you?"). She is the female Atlas, holding the world on her shoulders and yet she's always on time. Susan entered Spago in black pants, a matching suit jacket, and a white button-down blouse underneath.

"Diet Coke and a cup of coffee, black," she said to a waiter walking by.

Susan was my first friend in Los Angeles. It was a Saturday afternoon in August 1991. I had left Adam to go shopping by myself at the Beverly Center mall. I had just purchased a white off-the-shoulder cotton blouse (that I ended up never wearing) from Judy's, a cheapie-cheapie shop that later morphed into Contempo Casuals and was the only place I could afford to buy anything at the time. When I got home to our apartment, Adam was sitting on the couch talking with this attractive woman our age—twenty-two—in a pink Betsey Johnson Lycra flowered dress with a ruffled collar, black leggings, and a pair of motorcycle boots. I was instantly embarrassed by my cheapie-cheapie Judy's bag, which I immediately threw into our living room closet upon seeing that we had a Los Angeles stylish-looking guest.

Adam introduced me to our visitor. He knew Susan because she was the ex-girlfriend of a friend of his back in New York. She had this long dark spiral curly hair that she kept taking pieces of and wrapping around her fingers as she spoke. In the first five minutes that I knew her, Susan did all the talking. She was in the middle of a conversation with Adam about how she had just endured a year of recoup from a back operation and how angry she was with Columbia University because she was three credits short of graduating and how she was going to have to take a course that fall at a college in Los Angeles. "If it was a *man* who had this back problem," she'd surmised, "I bet you *anything* that they would have just had him write an essay about it and then just given him the degree for all he'd been through. But because it's a *woman* . . . !" She was brash, and a bit combative. In the hour she spent in our apartment, each seemingly harmless topic that was brought up always ended with her saying, "If it was a *man* . . ." or "But because it's a *woman* . . ." And I would nod my head in agreement, but in actuality, I disagreed with her and disliked this loudmouth objector very much. It was only when Adam left the room at one point that she turned to me and confided, "When I saw you come in, I saw that you got something from Judy's. Have you noticed by any chance that the fashions in this city suck?"

"Yes, I have!" I exclaimed.

"For men it's fine, T-shirts and jeans," she said.

"I know!" I agreed, getting wound up, "But for a *woman* . . . !"

From that moment on she was my feminist icon.

Twelve years have softened Susan, gearing that oomph in other directions, or maybe she's just too tired for the more trivial things in life.

As we kissed hello and she took a seat, I noticed some spit-up from one of her twins sitting on her lapel. When I mentioned it to her, she feebly dabbed at it, laughing. "Hey, it's cheaper than a brooch."

Felicia entered the restaurant next, dressed in a teal-colored wrap dress, her auburn hair cut into a classic bob. I noticed she had a large, dark blue box that she needed to carry with both hands, the word PRADA stamped on the ribbon that tied the box together.

Susan and I met Felicia during the Los Angeles riots in April 1992. With the fear that the whole city would burst into flames, I grabbed two bathing suits, some sweats, and my hair dryer and we headed down to a friend's parents' beach house in Malibu, where we spent the next five days in the lap of luxury, trying not to think about what was happening to our newfound city. It was unanimously agreed by everyone that Felicia would get the master bedroom on account of the fact that her boyfriend had just admitted to being a drug addict. Back at their apartment in Westwood, the guy was much more concerned about where he would find his fix, since his normal outpost had just been set ablaze in the uprising. Felicia had fled the apartment and come to Malibu. Given the circumstances at the time, my sensitivity level was on high alert, and any problems anyone had, even a stranger, were top priority. I spent the next five days pampering her, telling her she was a special woman, and that she could do much better than that guy.

Felicia has brought this up countless times over the years. Something about my concern meant Felicia was always wanting to say thank you for being there that time when she really needed someone. Because she feels indebted, Felicia has taken on this solicitous mothering aspect in our relationship. Sometimes I accept it and actually seek it out. Most times, it really grates my nerves.

We'll be in a store, for example, and I'll pick up an item. "What do you think of this?" I'll ask her.

"It's great!" she'll say. "You want me to get it for you?"

Now, I have a job; I'm not destitute. Why does she feel the need to pay for my lavender soap just because, fifteen years earlier, I comforted her when she found out her boyfriend was a drug addict? She does this constantly. Don't get me wrong, I love this woman and it's a beautiful thing, her always wanting to do something special, but as the chick that has already flown three thousand miles from the nest and given her parents' credit cards back, let me see the error in my ways, realizing the stupidity of buying a forty dollar bar of soap.

Back at the restaurant, Felicia handed me the Prada box as I gave her a sigh and said, "Honey, why would you do that?"

"Don't get mad at me," she said, curling her short auburn tresses behind her ear, "I just figured birthdays only come around once a year."

Heidi entered next and, as usual, she was a tornado of electric energy. A former ball-busting talent agent, Heidi and Susan met through work and after a drink with us one night, she became an instant part of our clique. Eventually, Heidi left her job to become a stay-at-home mom to her three children. With all the vigor she put into being an agent, Heidi put that same energy into her family and friends. If you didn't know it, you'd think she had three arms. She's the soccer-mom version of a chef at Benihana. Heidi can whip up the most gorgeous dinner party in seconds flat while teaching one of her three children the ABC's and talking on the phone with me, giving the most excellent advice on how to handle my boyfriend du jour. The same can be said for her wardrobe. I've always admired Heidi's wardrobe. She's comfortable yet chic—a jeans-with-a-frilly-top, dress-pants-with-a-T-shirt kind of gal. Heidi is the one I borrow clothes from the most and vice versa, though no matter what, there's usually a problem, a fight ensues, and we never learn from the mistake.

I once lent Heidi my brand-new Donna Karan black knit slip dress. She was really sweet and had had it dry-cleaned, but when it came back, something in the fabric had burned away and the dress became transparent. For lack of anything else, I decided to wear it to Julie Pelagatti's rehearsal dinner back in Philadelphia. A week later, Julie called me, frantic, saying that since I had gone sans bra, every picture that was taken of me showed my breasts— nipples and all—in full view. I gave Heidi a lot of objectionable guilt over that. After all, it wasn't her fault, it was the dry cleaners'. I got mine, however, when I decided to borrow her wool Burberry shawl, this amazingly warm yummy-thick wrap with the Burberry plaid all over it in shades of brown that could dress up any outfit while giving you the utmost in comfort. When she lent it to me sometime in February, I kept it much longer than I promised. When I finally decided to give it back in June, I thought it was only right to have it dry-cleaned.

Upon presenting it, she looked at it and said, "Now we're even; the dry cleaner got the fringe all frayed!"

Which it was. Not terribly, but a bit frayed nonetheless. And I said, "So you don't want it anymore?" thinking about my glamorous future in fully owning that scrumptious piece of coziness.

"Of course I want it," she grumbled, "but just know that when you feel like bringing up that stupid see-through Donna Karan dress story, you ruined something of mine, too!"

So now we're even.

One story I still have in my guilt files, though, happened at our friend Rachel's wedding, when Heidi borrowed another dress of mine (which we both agreed she would not be getting dry-cleaned upon return). I'm a little smaller than Heidi, though Heidi thinks I'm way smaller than her. Truth be told, Heidi's got big boobs and I don't, which makes me look smaller than her. Rather than enjoy the compliments of guests at the wedding on how pretty she looked, Heidi greeted each acquaintance with the words, "This is Adena's dress! Can you believe that I fit into it?" If she had said it, one, two, even three times, that would have been fine. Every time I turned around, there she was pointing at me and telling some stranger, "It's that tiny girl's dress, and it fits me! Can you believe it?" I even pulled her aside at one point and said, "Could you please stop saying that?"

"What?" she said. "It's a compliment!"

We didn't speak for a few days after that. Years later, I'm still not sure if I should have taken that comment as an insult or a compliment, though the way it made me feel, it's the former.

Heidi had four wrapped boxes in hand that she hurled at me as she kissed the other girls hello, picked the seat she wanted, grabbed a piece of bread, dipped it in olive oil, and popped it into her mouth.

"Open these three boxes first," she mumbled through her bread-full mouth while laughing.

I took the biggest one first and carefully unlaced the meticulously tied ornate gold ribbon and matching paper she had decorated the box with.

"Oh, just rip it open already," she said as she dipped her napkin in some water and went at Susan's spit-up brooch.

The first box held three T-shirts I'd lent her months before.

The next box held a pair of pants I'd badgered her at least five times to return.

The third, two pairs of my earrings I'd lent her years ago and thought I'd lost.

I looked at her with confusion.

"I wanted to make sure you started off this year with everything your heart desired."

"Awwww" and "shucks" filled the group, but Heidi was already off the subject, calling the waiter over and ordering a bunch of appetizers from the menu for everyone at the table to share.

Serena arrived next. She kissed everyone hello and took a seat next to me.

"Is this OK?" Serena asked, pointing at her outfit.

"Yes, is this OK?" I asked, pointing at mine.

"I love it," she said, pointing at mine.

"Are you sure?" I asked, pointing at mine.

"Positive. Are you sure?" she asked pointing at hers.

"I'm sure."

If Heidi is the one I borrow from the most, Serena is the one I mull over clothes with the most. Serena was introduced into our group of friends along with Heidi in 1992. They were working at the same talent agency. Serena is my straight-up soul sister of shopping. I actually knew what Serena would be wearing when she entered the restaurant that night: black jeans and a black see-through top with a camisole underneath and black boots. I always know what Serena is going to wear and vice versa. We understand each other's anxiety in the fear of wearing the wrong thing. In all other areas, Serena is a no-nonsense chief of . . . well . . . serenity. If I were on the phone with her and she suddenly had a problem, whatever it was, she'd be calm about it. "You know what, Dean?" she'd say tranquilly from her cell phone. "Let me call you back. There's a man pointing a gun at me through my car window." Or, "Wait, let me call you back, my daughters are throwing knives at each other."

Take the crisis of what to wear to an upcoming event, and it's mass hysteria.

"Code red! I have a wedding in three weeks!" she'd shriek.

"Black tie, cocktail attire, business attire, or casual?" I'd cry.

"Business attire!" she'd scream. "Who wears business attire to a wedding?"

For the next three weeks, people at work know why my head is cloudy.

"Who has the party to go to?" they'll ask. "You or Serena?"

In the anxiety of the frenzy, small boutiques, department stores, dressmakers, and fashion experts are shopped and consulted. Magazines and books are researched; friends' closets are ransacked for the perfect outfit. Notes are taken, clothing is tried and retried, backup safety outfits are bought and, when no outfit is set in stone, frustration sets in and an incident that happened years ago is undoubtedly brought up.

Years ago, as Serena would tell you, I made a faux pas. I still don't think I blundered, but when the frustration hits, she never fails to bring it up. For example, we've finally found what might seem to be the perfect business attire outfit.

"Are you sure about it, or are you just getting tired?" she asked.

"I'm sure."

"Are you positively sure?"

"I'm positively sure."

"SURE?"

"SURE!"

"BECAUSE REMEMBER THAT TIME?" she'd shriek, her long auburn hair becoming disheveled and unusually out of place.

This is what happened: Serena and I were both attending an awards ceremony, and because I had been to the same event the year before, I used my previous experience and said, "Everyone wore short dresses; don't even bother looking at the long ones."

When we got to the ceremony, I wore a short dress, Serena wore a short dress, the woman sitting next to me at my table was wearing a short dress, each of the women accepting awards wore short dresses, and if I had known this incident was going to affect me ten years later, I would have taken a count of the *rest* of the room and had it notarized, because Serena remembers that night otherwise and I've never heard the end of it.

"REMEMBER THAT TIME? EVERYONE WORE LONG DRESSES!" she'll say. "I FELT COMPLETELY UNDERDRESSED!"

"YES, I REMEMBER THAT TIME!" I'd yell back at her, "BUT I'M TELLING YOU NOW, THE OUTFIT YOU CURRENTLY HAVE ON IS BUSINESS CASUAL! NOW BUY THE STINKING OUTFIT AND LET'S BE DONE WITH IT!"

She'd buy the dress and, once again, peace would be restored in Los Angeles. I'd go back to my life; Serena would go back to hers.

And then, as it usually happens, twenty minutes before the wedding, Serena will call and say in her standard composed voice, "You know, I think I'm just going to wear that ruby dress I got last year. You know, the one with the frilly cap sleeves?"

A week later, I'd go to my mailbox and see an eggshell-colored envelope with calligraphic print on it.

The alarm sounds once again and Serena kisses her husband and children good-bye.

"What kind of attire did she say the invitation gave?" her husband would ask as she threw together an overnight bag of possible outfits for me from her own closet.

"Casual black tie," she'd say, then drive off to my apartment.

Rachel, the last of my five, entered, typically, last. I actually knew of Rachel, since we were both from Philadelphia, but we had gone to different schools, so while we knew of each other, we were never friends. It wasn't until 1992 that I got acquainted with her. She was the roommate of Susan's boyfriend at the time. Rachel became our sixth in the clique due to the fact that she was always able to report the whereabouts of Susan's boyfriend. The boyfriend is long gone, but we kept Rachel. Sometimes I joke that I met Rachel last because she was stuck in some store trying to figure out if she should buy the same T-shirt in white or white. Before anyone starts to think that Rachel's problem is the same problem that Serena and I have, you must understand it is enormously different. With Serena and I, the problem is only reserved for special occasions. With Rachel, however, I don't know how she fit the time in to have a powerful job, get married, and have a baby. I always say she's lucky she's got gorgeous natural ruby-colored hair. Otherwise, she'd never get out of a hair salon because she'd never be able to decide on a new color.

"Sorry I'm late," she said, handing me a gift. "I just couldn't decide what to get you."

We all knew. If Rachel was going to buy a simple birthday gift, knowing our reservation was at eight, she must have left her house to start shopping for the gift at about 3:30 that afternoon. This is the one thing about Rachel that bugs everyone to no end. Everything else about her is the greatest. She always has the best gossip, she's the first one to pick you up from the service station when your car breaks down, and once she made me laugh so hard I got kicked out of a restaurant for making too much of a ruckus.

But all of that aside, Rachel is the worst person to shop with. Rachel is a looker, a feeler, a browser. With the exception of an important occasion, I am a buyer: I see something, it fits, I buy it. Rachel has to look at every item in the store and check out its merits one by one.

One Saturday, for example, Rachel called and asked if I'd

come with her to buy a pair of black rayon pants. Instinctively, I gave her a flat "absolutely not."

"I swear," she said, " I know exactly what I want; it's going to take two seconds. I promise you we'll be in and out."

I looked at my watch. We entered the Beverly Center mall at exactly 1:42 and by 2:01, Rachel had found the pants she wanted in her size.

"I'm just going to try them on for you," she said. "Just two seconds, I promise."

Three hours and six stores later . . . Rachel hadn't realized that the first pair had a button; she preferred a snap. She felt the second pair made her butt look huge. The third pair had a static-cling problem. The eighth pair just didn't feel right. The ninth pair had a cuff and, two hours after that, just as the stores were closing, Rachel finally found the pair she was looking for.

I grabbed the pants and went to stand in line, but Rachel tugged back. I could see her mind in deep thought over the pants, feeling the texture of the fabric and squinting for any irregularities in the stitching. Was the fabric up to her standards? How would these pants benefit her life? Would they be useful? Would they pack easily? What was the update on the situation in the Middle East and, if she went to help, could she wear these pants?

I was becoming exasperated. I knew that this could be the end of our friendship. After ten years of being friends, someone would ask me why we weren't friends anymore and I'd have to tell them, "We went shopping."

At 5:57, Rachel and I finally left the Beverly Center. Rachel did not buy a pair of pants. I, on the other hand, did pay for the parking. Rachel forgot her wallet at home.

As we approached my house, she turned to me and said, "Look, I'm really sorry. I want you to know how much I really appreciate your coming with me."

"Whatever," I said as I opened the door to get out.

"I'll make it up to you," she told me. "I swear. We'll go to the Barneys sale tomorrow; it's the last day."

I thought about it for a second.

"OK," I said.

The next day, Rachel and I took separate cars and met at the Barneys sale. I was there for one hour and I bought two pairs of pants and a sweater. That was at one in the afternoon. At seven that night, Rachel called me on the phone and said, "Listen, I'm still here, I need you to do me a big favor and go over to my house and feed my cats. They haven't eaten all day, and I don't know when I'm going to get back there."

As the waiter came to take our order, he approached Rachel first.

"I'm not sure yet," she said, looking over the menu. "Start on that side," she said, pointing at Susan.

"Steak, medium-well—just a little pink in the middle—and a chopped vegetable salad."

"Would you like the salad dressing on the side?" he asked her.

"And why would you ask me that?" she questioned.

He didn't answer, not wanting to insult her by saying he assumed she was the stereotypical woman on a diet.

The waiter turned to Felicia, who turned to me. "Adena, would you like to split a pizza to start?" Then she turned to Heidi and said, "Heidi, I know you love the Dover sole, but I just noticed that it has cilantro on it, and I know you hate cilantro, so I thought I'd warn you before."

"Thanks for the warning," Heidi deadpanned as she turned to the waiter. "I will have the Dover sole, no cilantro, and a side of spinach."

"I don't really care what I have," Serena said to the waiter. "Make it your choice," she said, turning back to me.

By the time the waiter got to Rachel again, she still couldn't decide, and other tables were starting to pester the waiter.

"She'll have the special pasta," Heidi said.

"Let her do what she wants; she's a grown woman," Susan said.

"Split the pizza with Heidi and me," Felicia said.

"She'll decide when she decides," Serena calmly said.

Pretty soon, the waiter had served our drinks and we toasted to friendship. There were two working mothers, two stay-at-home moms, one woman with a serious boyfriend, and one single woman. Years before, for whatever the reason, we'd all arrived separately and alone in a new town. We threw on cheap Lycra flowered cotton dresses and we found our kindred spirits. Our new lives had affected our fashions and we had affected one another. For better or for worse, they were my second family, biggest influences, and soul mates for life.

A Change in Style

've never been one for loving change.

When Estée Lauder changed the formula on my favorite self-tanner, I called the company and demanded to speak to whoever was in charge. I'm still on hold. When Lancôme discontinued my favorite Matte Royale lipstick, I was ready to stage a sit-in. When Calvin Klein stopped making my favorite white cotton ribbed tank tops (aka "wife beaters"), in a pathetic attempt at salvaging, I braved the bemused look on my dry cleaner's face as I began getting my remaining stash dry-cleaned.

So in the mid- to late nineties at age twenty-seven, sans college sweetheart, I was beyond depressed, prophesying a morbid future. Alanis Morissette's *Jagged Little Pill* album had become my anthem. I had Counting Crows' "Anna Begins" playing on a loop. I felt like a sentence had been handed down to me.

"Miss Halpern," the judge of relationship court said as he threw down his gavel, *"you have been found guilty of finding the*

wrong man. You will be sentenced to a new life of pitiful blind dates, trivial conversation, boring parties, going dutch, one-night stands, notoriously awful dating tips, going to movies alone, sleeping alone, eating alone, simply being alone, and no one will bring you soup when you are sick. May God have mercy on your soul."

To add to the angst, the five women you meet in Los Angeles were all either in serious relationships or married with kids. I had to get cracking if I was going to catch up with them so we could all buy houses on the same cul-de-sac and walk our kids to school together, and they were more than keyed up for the task of helping.

"I think I've got the guy," Rachel announced, calling me from the supermarket. "I was standing here trying to decide if I should get Coke, Pepsi, Diet Sprite, Diet Dr Pepper, or Mr. Pibb and this guy turned to me, looking as perplexed as I was, and said, "There's so much to consider. I wish I could find a woman with a strong decision-making sense."

"I met him," Heidi said as I sat down with her and her daughter Sienna for lunch one day. "The only problem is that he likes tall brunettes," she said, staring at my blond hair, then tying Sienna's shoes and grabbing a toy for her to play with. "I figure he'll love your personality so much, he won't notice the blond or the height."

"OK," Serena said as we compared nail polish colors for an upcoming cousin's bar mitzvah, "the search is over. I found him."

His name was Billy Lange and he was, as Serena described, "a screenwriter on the verge of superstardom."

"Yeah, Billy Lange," he said as he picked up the phone, noticeably leaving out the "it's" in "It's Billy Lange," or "Hi, Adena. I'm Serena's friend Billy Lange." No, it was "Let's meet for a drink, say, Friday, Four Seasons Hotel. Seven o'clock. I've got brown hair. See you there."

Serena said that Billy Lange had really bad phone manners, but was actually a really good guy. "He must have been nervous," she said.

Serena arrived at my house on Tuesday at five o'clock. We had three days and two hours to get ready.

Serena flipped through my closet. The promise in potential guys was certainly there, but there was a much more delicate matter to attend to: My depression had affected my wardrobe.

"Where's the sexy stuff?" she asked, flipping through each hanging object as her eyes went wide. "Come to think of it, I can't remember the last time I saw you wear anything sexy."

As common as the notion for a twentysomething woman might be when searching for new clothes, the notion of "sexy" did not make it into the final analysis for me when buying something new. While quick tallies of fashionable, classy, fun, or cool did factor in, sexy wasn't even an afterthought. I had been in a relationship for so long, and then had been mourning the loss of the relationship for so long, I had lost the ability to think of sexy anymore in terms of clothing. For me, the mid-nineties were all about long, baggy, depressing dresses and skirts. I had resigned myself to the flowered dress, the frilly skirt, and the pencil-straight ankle-length skirt. Frankly, I looked like a "Before" picture.

"What about that black dress?" I asked, pointing to a sleeveless black jersey ankle-length dress with a scoop neck.

"Jeez, Dean," Serena said, pulling out the black jersey dress. "No offense. It's sexy if you're going to a funeral, but not for a date."

"Now I have to get a new wardrobe?" I cried like the eggshell I'd become.

"No, no, no," she said, taking a closer look at the dress. "We just need to sex up what you already have. This is a good thing." She handed me a tissue. "You're young; you need to have some fun. A change will do you good."

Off to the tailor we went. With my six-inch heels in hand, Serena and the tailor shortened the dress a little bit, then a little bit more, and then a little more than that, until I was left with a tiny black minidress. Cost for my new look: $8.

I felt incredibly uncomfortable heading on my first date out of the single file gate. I was sure that the tailor had made my dress too short. Did my minidress with the addition of my six-inch heels make me look like a hooker?

"I swear," Serena said, "you do not look like a hooker. You don't have enough makeup on to look like a hooker," she said as she dabbed a little rouge on my cheeks.

I didn't feel sexy at all. I felt awkward and agitated. I didn't want to date. I didn't want to see the world. Even though I was incredibly unhappy, I had gotten used to being unhappy. That was better than anything new.

"You're gorgeous," Serena said, trying to psych me up. "You've got great legs and a great figure. It's about time that you showed it off."

I entered the Four Seasons Hotel at exactly 7:17 p.m. I wanted to be a little late, and the two sevens I saw on my car's digital clock seemed like a lucky time to start my single life.

I stood in the entryway of the bar, trying to size up any man with brown hair who looked like he was a screenwriter on the verge of superstardom. There weren't any, so I got a glass of Merlot (the mid-nineties drink of choice) and took a seat at the bar. Sitting on such a high seat caused me to think that maybe my cellulite would be showing, so I took a seat on one of the couches— also a bad idea. Had Billy Lange sat down next to me on the sofa, I would have had to speak to him facing sideways. Keeping a short skirt from showing cellulite while sitting sideways felt like a disaster in the making, so I got up and switched to a regular chair.

"Hey, Goldilocks. Is that chair just right?" said a brown-haired guy who looked like he was a screenwriter on the verge of super-stardom sitting four feet away. I went red in the face.

"I hope you're Adena," he said, taking a seat on the sofa next to me. "Even if you're not, those are some great gams."

The limbs that held up my body were great? Those toned, lean things?

"Oh, goodness, thank you," I exhaled, crossing one great gam over the other and taking a sip of Merlot. "Genetics," I joked.

Four hours, three Merlots for me, and three vodkas on the rocks for him later, we were both drunk and if my cellulite was showing, I had no tact left to know or care.

The following morning, he left my apartment at about seven. Serena had to pick me up to take me back to the Four Seasons to get my car, but I told her we were going shopping first. If it was sexy, I was going to buy it. I came home that day with three pairs of skintight jeans, two miniskirts, four halter tops, a slinky slip dress, another pair of six-inch heels, and a hot pair of dangly earrings. The long skirts were put in the back of the closet for posterity.

"Are you going to see him again?" Serena asked me when I left her.

"There's a whole world of guys out there that I've never met," I said smugly. "Why would I want to just stop with the first one?"

The Knockoff

On my mother's first weekend as a freshman at the University of Pennsylvania in 1955, fourteen boys called to ask her out. Not five or six or seven or eight, but fourteen! Can you imagine?

"It was different in those days," Arlene would say with a shrug. "You went on a date without the notion that it might lead to marriage. You went to a dance hall together or you had a burger." Regardless of how she tried to downplay it, the volume was mesmerizing any way you looked at it.

"Get to the part when all the boys called," I'd say.

"Well"—she'd smile devilishly as her eyes sparkled—"the phone would ring and your grandmother would shout out, 'Here's another one!' "

I always loved the image of my mother jumping down the stairs in their Wynnefield home and grabbing the phone in the kitchen, acting so casual, as if each boy was the first to call.

"Friday night?" she'd repeat as my grandmother, Esther, stood listening in incredulity. "I'll have to check my calendar and get back to you."

I imagined my mother getting tired of taking the calls and Esther taking them for her, like her manager who would start to get picky with the boys, asking them something like, "You want to take Arlene out on a date Friday night? What did you say your major was? English literature? No, I don't think so. We already have a pre-law set up for that night. Change your major and get back to us."

"Did you sleep with any of them?" I'd ask.

"Of course not," she'd answer as if I'd offended her. "It was the fifties!"

"Did you wear something sexy that day?"

"For Christ's sake, Adena, it was the fifties," she'd say, getting pissed off. "The sexiest I ever got was keeping the top button open on my cashmere sweaters."

As the story went, it took her half the semester to go on a date with all of them, but she didn't end up marrying any of them and she never mentioned that she even seriously dated any of them.

This story has had a profound affect on my life. Never have fourteen boys at a time, much less five, asked me out in a single day. I know this is an impossible notion for anyone, but when you know the ability is in your blood, you might like to think you could come close.

After my one-night stand with Billy Lange, I realized that there was a whole world of dating out there that I had never even attempted to conquer in short black dresses and six-inch heels. The five women you meet in Los Angeles had that time while I was still with my college sweetheart five years out of college. This was my time, *my* first weekend at Penn, and whether Billy Lange had written my number on a bathroom wall followed by the words "for a good time call . . ." or it started to get around that there was a new single girl on the scene, I'll never know. What I do know is that they started calling, which in turn, for the first time in my life, gave me the confidence to be as picky as I wanted to be. Men could come and go for the slightest reason. Who cared? Another one was bound to pop up at any moment.

First there was Rob who called me "Little Heather Locklear" because of my blond hair, six-inch heels, and newly acquired short skirts, which he thought were reminiscent of *Melrose Place*. The Locklear comparison earned him a month of dating until I met Stu, who asked all five feet of me if I had ever modeled. That got him sex the very first night and a month and a half of dating until I dumped him for Andy, who sought me out at a party introducing himself and saying I was "a vision in red leather pants and a gray tank in a sea of black." That relationship only lasted two weeks, as I ran out of colorful clothes.

If I knew I was going to sleep with Bobby on the third-date take-out Chinese and DVD at his place, my outfit was always my slouchy Levi's with my best Calvin Klein ribbed white tank (the one that was the same as all the others, but for some reason looked better).

"Your arms look amazing in this," Bobby said as he slipped it off of me.

If it were a conservative guy, like Richard, I'd wear a black low-cut blouse, black cigarette pants, and pearls.

"The thing I like about you," Richard said, "you're conventional, but with a sexy edge."

If we were going to a business function, like the one I went to with Leo, I wore my Diane Von Furstenberg wrap dress for the I-just-came-from-work look, even though I'd secretly left work early to shower and put on my sexy wrap dress.

"There is no one sexier than you," Leo whispered before introducing me to his boss.

If a cute guy happened to come into my office and asked if I wanted to grab a drink after work, I kept a drawer at my desk full of accessories, which came in handy when I met Oliver.

"You're like an article in one of those fashion magazines," he said, complimenting the scarf I'd fashionably tied around my neck as he quoted, "How to turn your daytime outfit into night in two simple steps."

If it were a daytime activity date, like the time I went Rollerblading with Keith, I wore my black leggings, a white tank top, and my old gray long-sleeve Rolling Stones Steel Wheels Tour T-shirt that I stole from my brother David, which I wrapped around my waist.

"You're a sexy tomboy," Keith said as we skated off the cement path and fell into the grass. I had to give up that relationship the day he asked if I wanted to go swimming. He was cute, but not cute enough for me to get my hair wet.

Saturday night dates were all-embracing: my gold halter top with my Theory shiny black tight-fitting tuxedo pants. At a dinner party with Zach, Zach's friend Leslie kept gushing over the top.

"I am dating the sexiest, best-dressed girl in town," Zach boasted.

Black-tie events, like the one I went to with Al, called for my silk charmeuse slim-fitting white skirt and a black halter top with a V-shaped back.

"You look like someone Frank Sinatra would sing about," Al said as he dipped me on the dance floor.

Sometimes relationships ended simply because I had nothing else to wear, like when my relationship with Nick ended because I had worn the same outfit on date two as I did on date seven.

"I love the way you dress," Nick said when he picked me up for date two—dinner and a movie.

By the time date seven rolled around, I was out of the outfits that fit the criteria of the look he loved, so I put on date two's outfit and hoped for the best. He said nothing when I answered the door. He kissed me hello and complained about the traffic. I felt dirty. I had failed. Before he could get to it, I broke it off the next day using the old "things at work have been crazy/it's not you, it's me/I'm really screwed up right now/I'm not in the right place" excuse.

Sometimes it wasn't easy keeping up the sexy/ultraconfident sexscapade.

There was the time I got my six-inch heel stuck in a street grate. As I pulled the wedged heel from the grate, the force of the action made me knock into Gil, who in turn hit his head on a street pole and passed out on the sidewalk, his head bleeding profusely.

"Is there any way I can reimburse you for this?" I asked Gil as he lay in the ambulance on the way to the hospital after coming to consciousness with the paramedics finishing the stitches.

While Myles thought it was hysterical, trying to be playful and accidentally unhooking my halter top and leaving me topless for about three seconds, long enough for everyone within eye reach of our dinner table to catch a glimpse of my braless breasts, it was the last I saw of him.

That story went along the same lines as my date with Lawrence. I went to grab my water glass and inadvertently knocked a full glass of red wine onto my lap. Since I was wearing a pair of extra-tight white pants and had decided to go sans underwear, it is my belief that I will never experience a more self-inflicted source of mortification than when I had to walk out of the restaurant with a tablecloth wrapped around my waist. Worse, Lawrence had light-cream-colored seats in his car and insisted that I sit on some plastic bags he found in his trunk. I never ordered red wine ever again and always decline it if it's ever offered. Some wine-snob dates have haughtily disapproved when I've ordered a Pinot Grigio with steak. If they only knew.

Tale of the Underwear from Target

When you're in the dating world, there is so much work in order to fake perfection. If you're not careful, you might miss something crucial along the way. Gone is the idea of not putting on a little lipstick, even if you're going to the 7-Eleven to pick up some Doritos for a late-night munch fest. Back is mascara at midnight. Gone is wearing the oversized sweats that don't show off your body when you're going to the gym. Back are the tight, uncomfortable leggings that make your butt look sexy (albeit giving you a wedgie) while gliding on the elliptical machine. Gone are the easy cotton Calvin Klein pullover sports bras for everyday use. Back are the lace bras with the underwire, which have a strong possibility of stabbing you in the boob should the protective covering fray. Gone are the days of wearing your glasses when you drive. Back is the inability to see the pedestrian crossing the street so the cute guy in the Porsche next to you will caution you with a beep, causing you to stop, smile a thank-you, get a number, get married, have kids, and get a dog and name him " 'Stigmatism" (Stiggy for short)—your little joke, of course, referencing the first time you met.

Felicia had fixed me up with this guy Mick. We had gone on a few dates and had a great time. When we went for sushi and he confessed his inability to use chopsticks, I claimed it was "adorable," thus leading us into a comfortable zone.

One Sunday, Mick needed a fold-up card table and chairs, so we decided to head to the Target in the San Fernando Valley. We stopped at Krispy Kreme, contemplated a Wendy's hamburger, but settled on fries and a Frosty. As our sugar highs deepened to schizoid proportions, we raced through the parking lot toward the Target store like wild boars stoned on crystal meth.

"Oh, remind me to get some underwear," I casually requested.

Mick halted in mid-sugar freakout.

"Hold on. You buy your underwear at Target?" Mick rhetorically chided.

I stopped, shuddered, and tried to cover it—badly. "No, of course not. What, are you nuts? I was just kidding. All this sugar is making me say crazy things."

We cruised the fold-up table section, contemplated an oak one, settled for plastic, but my mind was someplace else. It was a few yards away, in the Target lingerie section. My true bliss was hanging on a rack, albeit somewhat haphazardly, by the lucky ladies who had gotten there before me. So close and yet so far. My secret cheap thrill—Gilligan & O'Malley brand to be exact, 100% cotton, low-cut bikini with a full seat—comes in a pack of three. I'm wearing a pair right now (though I didn't get them that day).

Later that week, Mick and I went on a double date with Felicia and her boyfriend, Hal.

"I wish Felicia would wear sexier underwear," Hal thought out loud so Felicia would hear.

"How's this for sexy," Mick sarcastically commented. "Adena gets her underwear from Target!"

"No, I don't!" I cried, shocked and ashamed.

Later that night, I told Mick it was over. Mick had crossed the line. Now everyone would know. Felicia was always a big talker.

Heidi called me at eight the next morning.

"Felicia says you got this great underwear from Target. Which one is it?"

"Gilligan & O'Malley brand, 100% cotton, low-cut bikini with a full seat. Comes in a pack of three."

Later that week at a dinner party, Susan mouthed these words: "They are so comfortable." Next to her was her husband, Robert. "Thanks a lot," he deadpanned.

I had started a revolution.

A month later, Mick came to my house.

"You are a special person," he said. "Last night I took this girl out. We went back to her place. Things started to heat up. When she took off her skirt and I saw her underwear, I started to think, 'Why mess around with a knockoff when you might be lucky enough to be able to have the original?' I left right then and there."

"Was it Gilligan & O'Malley brand, 100% cotton?" I asked him.

"Low-cut bikini with a full seat. Comes in a pack of three," Mick said, adding, "do you think we could give it another try?"

"Why not," I told him.

A week later he showed up at my house for a date wearing a leather vest with no shirt on underneath.

I said nothing, claimed pneumonia, and stopped taking his calls.

A Democrat in Republican's Clothing

had decided to wear my beige shift dress with my six-inch-heeled snakeskin slingbacks on my blind date with Evan in early August 1998. I was fast approaching my thirtieth birthday, and the thought of not having anyone permanent in my life was starting to jolt the countdown on my spinster clock. The bigger problem was, there was no one who I really liked. I was fortunate enough to have been asked out on a lot of dates and had an active enough social life to have met all different kinds of guys. Still, there was no one. So when my friend Ian called and said that he wanted to fix me up with Evan, I was more than keyed up to go.

Evan was an investment banker. Ian said that he was exactly the kind of guy I would like—smart, confident, Jewish, funny, and most important, had the one quality I've always been attracted to: He could really wear a suit. If I stop to really ask myself why this has always been a plus for me, I know it can be attributed to the early mornings I'd watch my dad go off to the hospital in one of his gray, blue, or chocolate brown suits. It was six in the morning, and my father was headed off to perform one of his early morning surgeries, but he always wore a suit to work—gray or blue or chocolate brown with a white or blue oxford dress shirt and one of his many blue ties with varied prints of tiny polka dots or plaids. He'd come into my room while I was still sleeping; I could smell his hair spray—the Dry Look for Men—a scent I remain fond of for this reason. He'd lean over my bed, give me a kiss, and wish me a good day, and I'd find the energy to open my eyes just as he walked into my brothers' room, wishing them good days. There I'd see my daddy for the first time that day—crisp, clean, and more handsome than I'd ever see him at any other time in my life.

The same goes for my grandfather Frank when I would go to visit him at his accounting firm. I would run into his office to find my "Pop-pop" Frank, whose suits and dress shirts he had tailor-made in the finest fabrics, and there he was. The only thing about him that wasn't dapper and elegant was the wonderfully ecstatic smile on his face and his arms flailing at me just waiting to get his hands on me for a hug. I'd jump into his arms, and he hugged me tight as I'd play with the handkerchief neatly folded in his breast pocket. He'd carry me from office to office, proudly showing off his "littlest princess," as he called me.

So call it a daddy thing, call it what you will. I'm a huge sucker for a guy in a suit.

I thought the beige shift dress was a really good idea. Evan told me he'd be coming from his office and to please excuse his suit. I felt incredibly comfortable talking to him on the phone, and that in turn made me feel a little negligent in sexy attire. Also, I figured we'd match well if I wore something more conservative. After all, he did claim on the phone to be a "Democrat in Republican's clothing." Would a conservative investment banker appreciate my usual date look—tight cigarette pants, a flimsy halter top, and six-inch heels? Maybe if I was a gift some client had sent him as a thank-you. He'd want a woman to be as traditional- and sophisticated-looking as he was. That, and my usual conservative black-cigarette-pants-with-pearls outfit had a loose cuff on one of the legs, and I had sworn off my own sewing since prom night years before.

At eight o'clock that evening, Evan rang my doorbell. I undid the locks and began my ritual in opening the door for a blind date—asking God, Allah, Mother Nature, and Santa Claus, *"Please let this be someone I might like."* Everything was happening in slow motion as I opened the door and saw the arm of his gray suit, then his jacket lapel, his blue tie, his blue dress shirt, his deep green eyes. With the door pulled open, seeing him in full view, my very first thought was "a *hot* Democrat in Republican's clothing!" I didn't let on, though, as I gave him a warm smile. It was what he did next that, in all honesty, opened my bottle of crush. The guy gasped at me like he had never seen a vision of beauty so true and so meant to be.

And I knew he was full of crap.

And I loved that he was so full of crap.

Let's face the facts. Yes, I will admit that I looked attractive . . . for a job interview. My hair was slicked back into a severe ponytail. The beige shift did nothing for my figure. Why I didn't spend a little more time perfecting my makeup with the addition of even a dab of lipstick is still beyond me. To put it harshly, I was not gasp worthy.

So I outwardly ignored it.

"I actually just got home from work," I lied, knowing full well that I told him I was home already when he called on my cell two hours before. "Would you mind if I put on something more comfortable?" I asked him as I mentally surveyed my closet and quickly decided on my black Theory stretch cigarette pants and red ribbed tank.

"You look gorgeous!" he lied. "We're late for our reservation anyway."

I grabbed my mini backpack purse (as if I wasn't pathetic enough) and locked the door to my apartment. Evan and I walked to his car, a beat-up green Saab convertible, which looked exactly like my beat-up Saab, only mine had a hard top—an obvious sign if I ever saw one. I suddenly knew why I loved that he fake gasped. It was something that I would have done myself at the time had I been the guy at the door. He was the male Adena. And for that very reason, even though I had only known him for about five minutes tops, he was a potential finalist in the Mr. Adena Halpern contest.

He told me that he was taking me to the hot new sushi restaurant, the one I was dying to go to, the one he couldn't wait to try. As we drove over to the restaurant and the wind from the open top blew my severe ponytail into a spunkier up-do, Evan took moments throughout the five-minute drive to reenact his gasp, never saying anything, like he was stunned speechless from my splendor. Again, I worked feverishly to outwardly ignore it, but the more he fake gasped, the more my crush deepened and the more insecure I got.

What I really should have been doing all this time was telling him that I had already been to the hot new sushi restaurant and maybe we could think of another place. As we entered the restaurant, I had suddenly remembered the main attraction of hot new restaurants: hot young babes—model babes, babes in cigarette pants, flimsy halter tops, and long flowing hair. As the six-foot model/hostess with the black leather miniskirt and flawless body showed us to our table, my shift dress got baggier, my six-inch heels got shorter. When the gorgeous redhead at the table next to ours dropped her chopsticks and went to pick them up, both Evan and I took the opportunity to look down her V-neck shirt, which was giving way to her perfectly sculpted (only by genetics and not by a plastic surgeon) breasts, I could feel my own breasts bobbing against my knees.

"There are some really pretty women in here," I casually remarked to try to make him think I was the one woman in the entire world who didn't have a problem with other women who were better-looking than me.

"But I'm sitting with the prettiest," he said and smiled.

The ultimate bullshit artist. This was the man of my dreams!

I watched Evan pay the bill for our edamame appetizer, tuna roll, and eel sushi, and I thanked him with a kiss on the cheek. He wrapped his arm around my waist and pulled me in to him as we left the restaurant.

"Do you think we could do this again?" he slightly begged, leaning in as we pulled up to my apartment.

"I think that's possible," I said as I leaned in too.

The two "conservative" Jews kissed passionately, then got out of the beat-up green Saab convertible, his hand in hers.

"Good night," she said as she took her keys out to open her apartment door.

"Good night," he sighed as though he might have buttoned up his suit jacket, thrown on a fedora, and gone singing in the rain had there even been a slight drizzle when she shut the door.

And as I closed the door to my apartment, I contemplated the next move while throwing off the beige monstrosity, taking my hair out of the ponytail, and figuring out the sexiest outfit I had for the next date. If I had used my brain, I could have figured out that I didn't have to contemplate anything so fast. Knowing who I was at that time in my life, and he being the male Adena, I should have known it was going to take Evan six months before he finally called me for a second date.

Shopright.com

No matter what I ever do in my life as an occupation, there will never be a job better than the one I had from 1999–2001 with the Web site Shopright.com.

Here was the job: Shopright.com hired me to be their Los Angeles editor, which sounded super cool to those I wanted to impress. My "editing" job was to shop at every single upscale retail department store or boutique in all of Los Angeles and report on three designer items on sale in the store. For example:

> The Haute Store
> 888 Fabulous Boulevard
> Los Angeles, CA 99999
> (310) 555-5555

1. DKNY crochet poncho in lemon
   Was: $215
   Now: $179

2. Marc Jacobs denim jacket with pearl metallic lining
   Was: $357
   Now: $278

3. Robert Clergerie basic ebony-colored pumps with a round toe
   Was: $456
   Now: $378

Every time I reported on three sale items at a particular store, Shopright.com paid me $12.50. Think about it. Go to a sales rack in your favorite upscale retail store and write down everything that's on sale. Sometimes, I'd write down twenty pieces of clothing from one store, reporting it on Shopright.com, thus making $250 from one store. That's a half hour of work. Go to the next store, report on another ten pieces of clothing, and that was another $125. While the rule at Shopright.com was that we could only post three sales from one store per week on the site, it wasn't like the sale items were going away, and it wasn't our job to report if the item was purchased. Therefore, if you reported on twenty sales items, three would go up one week, followed by three the next, etc. I was making more money than you could imagine for doing something that took absolutely no effort, brain power, or skill. Because I worked from home, I had no one to report to and only worked about two hours a day, taking Fridays off entirely simply because I could. I almost felt like I was gypping the good folks at Shopright.com, but that was what they wanted. While I would have handled the business differently, that was not my problem. I was hired to shop and report, and $12.50 was what they offered for three sales items.

Needless to say, I took the job very seriously.

The reports were a free service for the shop owner, and when they started getting customers based on what I had reported on the Web site, the shop owners let me have whatever I wanted, sometimes at 50 percent of the cost. If a *lot* of people came into the store because they'd heard about it on Shopright.com, the shop owners would even give me an item of clothing I liked, free of charge as a thank-you. One place gave me a gorgeous pair of gold hoop earrings. Another gave me a cream-colored cashmere sweater, which I gave to my mother for her birthday.

Sometimes the shops didn't trust me and kicked me out of the store for writing down notes. The Powers That Be at Shopright.com advised that should something like that happen, I should tell the shop owners that I was just taking notes for a friend who really wanted those particular D&G jeans . . . and by the way also wanted that Rebecca Taylor silk top and those Prada boots in black. That didn't happen too often, though.

Another turnoff was when I walked into some boutique that never got any customers, especially, say, at four in the afternoon on a Wednesday. All the salespeople wanted to do was talk about nothing of any importance, and they wouldn't give me a second to write down any sale items. I avoided those places.

The Powers That Be at Shopright.com were upset with me twice. The first time was when I was reprimanded for concentrating on Los Angeles stores and disregarding the San Fernando Valley. Truthfully, the thought hadn't occurred to me, so I added the Valley to my route.

The second time Shopright.com lectured me was when a rule came down that colors could not be described with their basic names. They felt that clothing didn't sound as glamorous, and I was right on board with that idea. Instead of saying beige, for example, they asked that you say "camel." If the article was blue, you should say "sapphire" or "azure." I got really into naming my colors and got a little too carried away. They drew the line when I referred to a blouse in yellow as "black-and-blue-mark-after-a-week yellow," or saying that a charcoal gray suit jacket came in a shade of "my friend Jimmy's dirty kitchen floor."

I've never been a big sale shopper. I have no artistic eye for what the future could hold when looking at a pair of linen pants that have been crushed by the clothes surrounding them on one of those circular clothes-hanger merry-go-rounds. I've always been the type of person who needs to see it on the mannequin. I can't shop at Loehmann's, though I'm jealous of those who can. Because I had to do it for the job, though, everything was closely scrutinized and commented on when necessary.

For example:

1. Cynthia Rowley knee-length empire-waist silk spaghetti-strap dress in electric cobalt
   Was: $236
   Now: $156 (*Pssst . . . there's a little hole in the seam on the right side of the dress. See if they'll give you an extra discount.*)

The Powers That Be loved it when I did things like that.

The Return

Everything was going my way in the winter of 1999. I was actually using my gym membership, my hair had grown out from the last horrible haircut and, after a lifelong search for jeans that looked halfway decent on me, Theory introduced a wonderful pair of stretch jeans. Shopright.com not only paid very handsomely, but it also introduced me to all the salespeople in the best shops, thus giving me the unique opportunity of knowing when to be at the right shop at the right time when the hottest clothes came in or went on sale. This in turn made me a more desirable-looking object on the single scene.

It put my girlfriends' minds at ease as well. Heidi begged to borrow my Miu Miu multicolored three-quarter-length coat (which I'd really like back one of these days). When Rachel still couldn't find the black pants she needed, I recorded every pair of black pants I saw in her size and wrote up a report for her. Susan had no time to shop for the Women in Hollywood Luncheon, so I picked out a lovely DKNY pantsuit in gray and had it sent over to her. When Serena had a friend's thirtieth birthday party that called for "French Chic" attire, I knew the exact outfit she should get and we fixed the fashion emergency in a record ten minutes.

I was living in a utopian paradise except for one thing. What ever happened to that Democrat in Republican's clothing who fake gasped? I thought we had a connection there. Did I say something wrong that night? Was something in my teeth? Was my beige . . . er, camel-colored shift dress as awful as I thought it was? These were questions I posed in my mind from time to time as I drove from one upscale boutique to another.

Six months after our first date, I was taking notes on an Armani cap-sleeve dress in aqua (*Was:* $864 *Now:* $639) when my cell phone rang.

"Hi," a voice said apologetically, "remember me?"

"I'm sorry, who is this?" I feigned perfect ignorance.

"I'm sorry I haven't called sooner. Work has been nuts, my family is driving me crazy and, to be honest, I was dating someone and we just broke up."

"Me too on all accounts," I answered as I made a mental note to call the guy I was dating at the time to tell him it was over.

"So what's going on with you?" he asked.

"Oh, nothing much, I've been made the Los Angeles editor of an upscale fashion Web site called Shopright.com," I casually mentioned.

"Editor!" he exclaimed. "Wow, you're an editor! That's so cool."

"It's OK," I said with a pout. "I mean, the one nice thing is that I now know where all the hottest clothes are at the best prices."

"For men, too?"

"Oh sure. Men, women, children, dogs, ferrets . . ." I tried to joke, but it fell flat.

"Do you know the designer Dries Van Noten?" he asked.

"Oh sure," I answered confidently, since I absolutely did know who he (or she) was, or at the very least certainly, his (or her) designs.

"I have these awesome Dries Van Noten shoes in black that have this really comfortable rubber sole, and I really want to find them in brown."

"Oh sure," I said, unsure. "I think I know exactly where to find them. I actually have to go over to that store, so I'll look for you."

"Great. You can let me know when I see you on Friday."

"Friday?"

"That is, if you're free for dinner," he said as his voice softened.

"I'm free," I said, blushing.

"I really can't wait to see you," he said, possibly sincere.

"Me too," I said.

It was two days until the date. I had one day to dump the guy I was dating, get my hair done, get my nails done, get a facial, a massage, and contemplate Botox. The other day, of course, would be for finding those shoes . . . and, of course, finding out whether Dries Van Noten was a man or a woman.

Dries Van Noten Was
a Man of All Men

could not find a thing wrong with my Democrat who dressed like a Republican. Turned out he was really good at investment banking.

"Internet stocks," he said, "that's the way to go for a quick buck right now."

So I did.

And when he told me to sell, I did, doubled my investment, and bought him a Co-Op Harris Tweed blazer in mushroom as a thank-you, which he looked adorable in.

From his perfectly tailored Hugo Boss and Armani suits to his rugged jeans and the skull caps (which, by the by, he was sporting way before the craze started) that he wore on the weekend, anything he said or wore was right and just and warranted, because in my eyes this guy could do no wrong. While the overly romantic statements he'd make still gave rise to a small question of authenticity in the way back of my head, in time I was able to disregard my pessimism completely.

"I need to make out with you for at least ten minutes before we go to dinner," he'd say as he entered my door to pick me up for a night on the town. Then he'd take me in his arms and sink his lips into mine. It might have been a cool sixty degrees outside, but even in my skimpy sheet of a DKNY satin slip dress in sapphire, the way he wrapped his arms around me so tight and secure made me melt into a sea of balmy passion, and I felt like someone could have taken a picture and put us on the cover of one of those romance novels.

"I need a second of gorgeous," he'd say when he called me in the middle of a workday, much to my euphoric delight.

Even when he'd arrive at my house after working a twelve-hour day, to me, the wrinkles in his dress shirt or the ketchup stain he had on his jacket was the height of charming.

"How cute is this?" I'd say to Felicia. "He had a burger for lunch and the ketchup dripped on his jacket."

"Oh no," she warned jovially, "my little girl is in love."

"You're letting this guy get you too easy," Heidi said. "You need to play hard to get," she cautioned.

I was too far gone to listen to anyone's opinion at that point. I would have given him the safe combination to Fort Knox if he had asked me for it. I would have sold secrets to the Soviets. I would have told him who Deep Throat was, had I known at the time. In short, I was nuts for this guy.

He loved everything that I wore.

"Like a little French schoolgirl," he said when I went to visit him at his office in a pleated skirt and frilly white cotton blouse with a Peter Pan collar.

Or when he came over to watch a DVD and order Chinese:

"Damn, your ass looks fine in these Levi's," he said as pulled them off of me.

When we went to the theater, my Theory red-and-black flowered cigarette pants, DKNY black rayon sleeveless V-neck top, and especially-made-for-Bloomingdale's Tahari three-quarter-length jacket in black sparked a most welcome jealous streak in him. "I'm going to hold your hand all night so all the other guys know to back off," he said.

And I knew that he could definitely be *the* one when he said the kindest, most magical words every girl with high-heeled shoes on begs to hear: "I'm going to go get the car and bring it around so you don't have to walk so far."

When I checked every store in Los Angeles and the San Fernando Valley for those Dries Van Noten shoes in brown and came up empty, I went to him wary and apologetic.

"I can't even believe you were still looking for those," he said, throwing his suit jacket around my shoulders as we left a movie theater one chilly night. "I totally forgot about that. You know something?"—he stopped, pulling me in tight—"I think you are the most perfect woman in the world."

Was he out of his mind? How could this be possible? He liked me as much as I liked him? What were the odds? Had I become the cynical single gal that I was afraid of becoming? Yes, I had. Of course I had. How stupid could I have been that very first second we saw each other? That fake gasp was real! How could I have ever mistaken it for anything else?

I brushed his hair from his eyes, and he put his hands through mine and kissed me on the lips. Images of our future flashed through my head. Our wedding: I'd wear Vera Wang, of course. The birth of our children swaddled in cashmere blankets each time we left the hospital—the first one pink, followed by blue. Thanksgiving with my family back in Philadelphia in Ralph Lauren sweaters in an array of neutral browns, oranges, and tans would always be a photo fest, watching the children play in the leaves that so tidily matched their sweaters. My Internet stocks would come in even bigger, so vacations at our Aspen compound with matching blue-and-white ski suits and yearly Christmas holiday breaks to Hawaii in skimpy bathing suits with leis around our necks would always be the holiday cards that friends loved to get the most. "You have the picture-perfect family," they'd say. I was getting to imagining the end of the montage at our fiftieth wedding anniversary party ("I still gasp in awe at her beauty every time I see her," my black-tie-attired, graying love would say in his speech as our children and grandchildren dabbed their eyes). That's when a shiver of fear shot through my body, a huge pit formed in my stomach, and the montage faded to black. None of this would ever happen for one colossal reason: How on earth was I going to make my perfection charade last for fifty years?

The Liar, the Witch, and Her Wardrobe

My lies in the pursuit of perfection started out innocently.

"Cute underwear," Evan said. "Who makes them?"

"La Perla," I answered suspiciously.

"Are those six-inch heels?"

"Yeah, right," I scoffed with a nervous laugh. "Not Quite. Only four."

"Do you remember your prom dress?" he asked one day.

"Oh sure, did you ever see *Broadcast News*?"

Evan loved everything about me, and if he loved what he saw, then I couldn't let him down.

The thing was, I knew Evan wasn't playing some game with me, and that killed me to no end. When we spent the weekend together in Santa Barbara, he brought only a bathing suit, some extra underwear, and sunscreen.

"We're on vacation," he said. "You don't care if I wear the same thing every day, do you?"

"Heck no," I said as I watched him try to stuff my oversize suitcase into his trunk. Each day he threw on those same jeans, thermal shirt, and T-shirt, I felt such a hit of jealousy. He looked so comfortable, and all I wanted to do was wear the jeans and tank top I was wearing when we drove up. I just couldn't, though. In the nine months of dating, he'd never known me to wear the same thing twice, and he commented on it with friends, saying, "She's so up-to-the-minute in fashion that after she wears it, it's out of style."

We had been dating for about a year when he called one Saturday morning to extend an invitation from his boss to come to the boss's beachfront home in Malibu for a day of sun and surf. This was out of the question.

"You know what? I don't know what I ate last night, but my stomach is just going crazy," I said as I let out a little cough followed by a sniffle.

"Poor baby," he said, adding, "do you want me to bring you anything?"

"No, you go to your boss's. I'm just going to spend the day trying to get better."

"No," he whined, "I don't want to go without you. My boss wants to meet you. You think you'll be better by tomorrow? I'll tell him we'll drop by tomorrow."

Yes. I could be better by tomorrow. If I planned my Saturday wisely, by getting professionally fake tanned, followed by a trip to this great bathing-suit store in the Valley to pick up that gorgeous gold-and-black sheer coverup that would look perfect with my high-cut black one-piece and gold strappy Jimmy Choo heels, yes, I could be better by Sunday.

"I'm sure I'll be better by tomorrow," I told him. "I'm sure this is just a twenty-four-hour bug."

"I want you to lie in bed all day. Call me if you want me to bring some DVDs."

"No," I said with another sniffle, "I think I'll just sleep. I think I'll turn my ringer off too. You know, so I won't be disturbed. I'll call you later in the afternoon."

I left my house at about noon for my 12:15 appointment with the faux tanner. The trip to the bathing-suit store in the Valley took a little longer than I thought when I spotted another upscale boutique that I hadn't yet reported on. I didn't take my cell phone for fear that if anyone called, I might answer it and mention that I was in the Valley. The person would, with my luck, just happen to run into Evan and tell him they just spoke to me from some bathing-suit store in the Valley. I had all my bases covered.

I got back to my home at about five o'clock and opened the door, packages in hand, and there was Evan sitting on my couch with a Blockbuster bag sitting next to him.

"Where have you been?" he asked, looking a little closer at my orange tinted skin.

"I was feeling better so I decided to head out," I said as I quickly threw my packages under my dining-room table.

"Where'd you go?" he asked.

"Just to finish some work. I had some more work to do in the Valley, so I figured I'd get it done."

"And you bought some more clothes?" he asked, walking over to the table.

"It was on-*sale* on-sale," I lied as I wondered where I'd left the receipts. "Plus, they gave me even more off since I'd given them so much business."

"Why are you orange?" he asked, looking at me askew.

"They were having a promotion at the store: buy a bathing suit, get a fake tan." Lie upon lie upon lie.

"Well, I thought I'd surprise you, but I guess you're feeling better," he said, walking past me.

"Hey, what's the matter?" I asked him.

"I don't understand why you lied. You weren't sick at all."

"Hey, we didn't have plans today, " I reminded him.

"Because you were sick," he said. "But you've never looked healthier, albeit like a carrot."

"Well I'm sorry, I wanted to be alone!" I said, raising my voice at him.

"So be alone with all your clothes!" he shouted back as he stormed out of my apartment.

Why did I feel the need to buy all these clothes? Why was I trying to be someone that I wasn't? I felt like I had become a witch—the wicked bitch of the West. Why couldn't I just be myself, whoever she was at that point? I took out my new gold-and-black coverup and opened my closet, searching for a free hanger. There wasn't one, so I folded it up and left it on my dining-room table, where it sat for the next four weeks.

Evan called that night and canceled going to his boss's the next day. He needed some alone time too.

Babe and Hun

I t was four in the afternoon on a Thursday, and I was in Bloomingdale's at the Beverly Center mall, trying on some Theory stretch jeans and wondering if it was worth buying them since I owned a pair just like them. The difference between *my* Theory jeans and *these* Theory jeans was that there were no pockets in the back. I kept turning to look at my butt in the mirror, wondering if Evan would notice. I had worn my Theory jeans with the pockets in the back twice already with Evan and he commented on it. When I lied and told him I owned more than one pair, he appreciated the fact and said, "That's a really smart thing to do." Therefore, I had to spend $150 on another pair just so he wouldn't catch me in yet another fib.

I kind of liked the fact that there were no pockets in the back of these Theory jeans and wondered if I might want to crop them. I went back and forth with this idea and even contemplated getting two pairs—one identical to the pair I already owned with pockets in the back, and then a pair with no pockets that I would crop.

Whenever I go to Bloomingdale's at the Beverly Center mall in Los Angeles, no matter where I am in the second-floor ladies' section, I always head to the dressing rooms in the middle of the floor, right off the escalator. I like those dressing rooms because they have the best light. I hate the dressing rooms on the other side of the store to the far left. There's no light there, and I always end up buying whatever it is because I don't notice that the sleeves are too bunchy or the pants are too tight in a bad way, given the low light factor.

I decided that I would go out and grab another pair with pockets and try them on to buy just in case. This is the only problem about my favorite dressing room. Whatever I grab is usually on the side where the low-light dressing rooms are and I have to either put on my clothes again or trudge over there in whatever I've tried on. Forget asking a saleswoman; they're never around.

"Babe?" a male voice called through the slotted door.

"Yeah, Hun?" a female voice replied.

"They had it in a four."

"Oh, that's great," Babe said as I heard the dressing room door next to me open.

"I think the two looks fine, though," Hun said.

"I feel uncomfortable in it," Babe said.

"It looks all right to me," Hun said.

"I'll just try on the four and see how it looks," Babe said as I heard her dressing-room door close.

This conversation depressed me beyond belief. Why wasn't Evan here getting me the size four instead of two?

I got dressed, picked up my no-pocket Theory jeans, and walked out of the dressing room, where I found Hun standing. He was holding three other shopping bags from other stores in the mall. Tall and built like a football player, he had a really nice head of brown curly hair that needed to be shaped and cut. He looked like this was the last place he'd be in the world, like he should be at some bar drinking beer and watching a football game, but instead he was standing in the good-light dressing rooms at Bloomingdale's. Anything for the woman he loved. I called Evan.

"Hey, Hun," I said when he picked up the phone.

"Hi, Babe," he said.

"So, I was just at Bloomingdale's, and there was this really adorable couple next to me in the dressing rooms and I just suddenly missed you."

"Shopping again?" he said with a sigh.

"Well, it *is* my job," I copped as he sighed again. "What are you doing now?" I asked, quickly changing the subject.

"I'm actually getting some work done so I can get out of the office early," he said. "Let me call you later."

"We're having dinner tomorrow night, right?" I asked him.

He paused, and my heart stopped. "Yeah, sure, uh . . . I'm just in the middle of something though. Let me call you later."

"When is later?" I asked him.

"I don't know," he grumbled. "Later."

"Are you still mad at me?"

"I can't have this discussion now. Let me call you later."

And with that, he hung up the phone.

I rushed over to Susan and Rachel's office. A year before, Susan hired Rachel as her second in command, so it was much easier to huddle some girls when I needed them. They would know how to handle this. They knew how to take the mature feminine approach.

"He's just busy," Susan said. "People get busy. You've been busy, haven't you?"

"Not busy enough to let him know if I was angry with him."

"Maybe he's confused about things," Rachel piped in. "I mean, after all, you have been dating for a year, and neither of you are getting any younger. If I were either of you, I'd really take the time to see where this was going. That's probably what he's doing. Or maybe not."

"Well, we're having dinner tomorrow night and I have to look special. Does anyone want to come shopping?" I asked, looking straight at Susan.

"I actually need a new sweater," Rachel said.

"Susan?" I asked, ignoring Rachel.

"Why do you need to look so special all the time anyway?" Susan asked. "Lately, all you ever talk about is new clothes and what you're going to wear when you see him. To tell you the truth, I don't think this relationship is very good for you."

"He likes that about me!" I told her.

"Are you sure?"

"He thinks I'm perfect!"

"This isn't you, though. You're not this person who buys all these clothes and breaks plans because you need to have the right bathing suit."

"Look," I said staring at them, "you don't know what it's like anymore. Both of you are married with children. You don't know what it's like out here."

"Out where?" Rachel scoffed.

"In the single world!"

"Is that like the land of the living versus the land of the dead?" Susan laughed.

"And which land are we in?" Rachel joked, and they slapped each other a high five. I was in no mood for jokes.

"You don't know what it's like anymore to have to prove to some guy that you're the one for him because at any second, some girl who looks better in a pair of jeans, or worse, some girl with a better personality who looks better in those jeans is going to come along and steal your guy."

"But you're missing the point," Rachel said, taking my hand. "The guy who truly loves you is the one who makes you feel that any jeans are fine."

"That's great advice from the person who is worst at decision-making."

"In shopping, yes, but in life," she said, flashing her wedding ring, "obviously not."

I hated her very much at that moment.

"Take Robert, for example," Susan started.

"I've heard this. *'I was the fattest I ever was,'* " I said, repeating the beginning of the story I always loved to hear except now.

"Well, I was. I was the fattest I ever was, and Robert came to pick me up for a blind date and I was wearing this pink muumuu, and I looked like a pink powder puff and he didn't care."

"Well, you got the last one who didn't care."

"Honestly, I don't think that Evan cares either, but I think you're stuck in this idea that you have to be someone you're not."

"You know what?" I said, grabbing my bag and heading toward the door, "I don't need this. I don't need your advice when you have no idea what you're talking about anymore. I need some single friends." I grunted and stormed out.

What did they know? I decided I would not be talking to them for a while. Evan and I were hitting a glitch. "It happens in all relationships," I said to myself as I left my friends' office. Relationships can't always be all Babe and Hun. There's gotta be a Jerk and Witch in there too sometimes to make everything more even, and that's where we were.

Final Sale

You know when someone wants to break up with you. Even when friends tell you it's not going to happen, you know. It's that psychic seventh sense knowledge that you try to shove underneath the blankets, saying "It's all in your head," or "It's just a rough patch." None of it matters. You know very well that you're about to get dumped, and no matter what you do, what you say, or what you try to feel, it's all padding for the blow.

Having said that, I had decided to wear my new cropped no-pocket Theory jeans with a robin's egg blue–colored cardigan sweater and white T-shirt underneath for my dinner date with Evan. At five o'clock he called and told me that he'd rather stay in so we could "talk" rather than go to a restaurant. I told him it was fine and ordered Chinese, but truthfully it wasn't. That brief conversation earlier freaked me out to no end, and I had to make one last-ditch effort to try to get everything right. Each uncomplicated question was beyond my administrative ability with the Chinese place—"Dumplings fried or steamed? Shrimp or chicken with broccoli or both? White rice or brown?"—too many decisions, and why did my hair look so flat?

"I just feel like everything is life or death in this relationship," Heidi said when I called her in a panic. "Just throw your hair over and spray some hairspray in it. Brown rice is better for you. You've always liked shrimp better than chicken, so get that."

Evan arrived at my house in an Armani gray suit and white shirt at 7:30 on the dot, and the meal was waiting for him. As he finished his first spoonful of shrimp and broccoli, he sighed and turned to me.

"I just don't think I can do this anymore," he said.

"I was going to get chicken, but you know how I don't always trust chicken under brown sauce; you don't know what you're getting," I answered, praying for a glimmer beyond hope that this was exactly what he meant and we'd throw out the Chinese and order a pizza.

"No," he interrupted, "I mean, I just don't think we should see each other anymore."

I looked down at my sweater. There was a stray piece of rice on it, which I quickly picked off and got up to throw it in the trash.

"Did I do something to upset you?" I asked, looking for more stray rice on my sweater.

"No, it's not that, I just feel like"—he paused—"I just feel like we're not compatible. I know that's a clichéd thing to say, but I think it's true. The strange thing is that every now and then I see this part of you that I really like, but as the months go on, I feel like you're too much of a perfectionist. We've been together for a year, and I really don't know anything about you except where you bought tonight's outfit. I try and get to know you, but the more I do, I feel like this wall around you gets thicker and thicker. I'm just getting sick of it."

I couldn't say anything. I wanted to, but how do you tell a person that you've been dating for a year that you are truly a clumsy, bedraggled neurotic who never said or did one thing that wasn't well planned because you didn't want him to find out the truth?

"Do you remember the first time we went out?" he asked, not waiting for an answer. "I just remember you opening the door to your apartment and seeing this really beautiful woman who wasn't done up or trying to be something that she wasn't. You didn't seem like every other girl out there. I had seen you for all of two seconds and I truly thought to myself, 'This is someone I could see myself being with. This is someone just like me.' So then we went to that sushi place and I could tell you felt uncomfortable there and you looked it and, I don't know, I just loved that about you. I just thought it made you even truer. You were just being yourself. Most women would have tried to put up a front and get nasty, but you just said to me, 'There are a lot of pretty girls here,' and I just thought, 'You're the prettiest girl here.' You were the prettiest girl there because you were the truth. I'll be honest with you. It scared me that night. I really thought that you were the one for me. It scared me so much. That's the reason I didn't call you for six months. I tried to date other girls, but every time I went out with someone else, I came back home thinking of you."

His words stung like acid reflux from spaghetti sauce. His words broke me. From the very first second I saw him, all because of my own hangup, I saw what living a lie had done to us.

"I've been living a lie with you this whole year!" I shouted. "I thought you *liked* those girls. I thought I should *be* one of those girls!"

"Why, though?" he asked, "Why? I even told you one night that I thought you were perfect. Why did you feel like you had to change?"

I had no answer. Tears started streaming down my face. The mascara was also streaming down my face and onto my robin's egg–colored cardigan, and for once I wasn't about to get some club soda to try to take out the stain before it settled.

"You're just not who I thought you were," he said, taking my hand.

"But I am, I swear," I told him.

"Every time I see that closet of yours," he said, "that's all I know about you. I have no idea who you are underneath. Look, you're a wonderful person, but I just need to be with someone who I feel more comfortable with. I'm sick of trying to feel so perfect around you. I don't like the feeling that if I drop some ketchup on my jacket and I don't change, or if I wear the same thing on a weekend vacation, you're going to think less of me. I don't want to have to constantly keep watching what I say or do or wear. When you wouldn't come to my boss's house and lied to me about being sick, that was the end for me. I'm sorry for sounding cruel, but I want to be with someone who has more depth than that."

"I swear," I told him, "I'm all depth, I'm a pit of depth. Ask me. Ask me anything," I cried.

"It's just too late," he said, putting his arms around me as he gave me a good-bye hug. "I'm sorry. This just isn't working for me anymore. I'm going to go."

And with that, he put on his gray suit jacket and left my apartment for the last time.

I stood staring at the unfinished Chinese dinner. He had me all wrong. All I wanted to do was run out to him and dramatically bang on his beat-up Saab's driver's side window and cry out in a desperate attempt at reconciliation, "I KNOW PAIN! I SPLIT MY SHORTS IN THE SEVENTH GRADE! I HAVE FLAT FEET!" I didn't, though. It was too late for any of that.

He would never know the real reason behind the six-inch heels or the glorious comfort I felt from wearing a pair of Gilligan O'Malley underwear from Target. He would never know that I idolized Madonna or how many times my breasts had been accidentally exposed in public. He would never know that I had any quirks or funny thoughts or even a smart one now and then, because I never allowed him to. I was too afraid that once he found out what was underneath all the style and pizzazz, he might not have liked what he saw and in return, I ended up making him feel the same way. It's really a shame, too. We would have gotten along really well.

I picked up the phone and called Rachel and Susan, who came right over.

"So, you panicked," Susan said. "Big deal. Next time we'll warn you sooner. We'll shoot you up with some Ativan."

"Happens to all of us," Rachel said, putting her arm around me.

They stayed with me for the rest of night.

Two days later, I got a pink slip e-mail from Shopright.com. They were bankrupt and going out of business.

Juicy Couture
Black Linen Drawstring Pants

(2001–2002)

A pair of Juicy Couture black linen drawstring pants was laid to rest today after being battered and worn to their slow and painful demise.

With their early 2001 birth unknown (though tag records indicate MADE IN THE USA), the pants spent their early days in the spring of 2001 at the Barneys New York store in Manhattan.

"Yes, we have it in a small," a Barneys saleswoman said over the phone to a saleswoman at Barneys in Beverly Hills, followed by, "You're kidding . . . No, she did not. . . . She said what? . . . That is hysterical . . . Sure, I'll FedEx them today." The New York saleswoman then folded the black linen drawstring pants and put them in a FedEx envelope as she told a fellow Barneys saleswoman the story of the black linen drawstring pants' new owner in Los Angeles, California.

The new owner, described by the saleswoman in the Barneys Beverly Hills store was said to be a "miserable blond-haired woman in her early thirties" who tried on a pair in a size medium in the Beverly Hills store. Before buying the medium-size pants, she informed the saleswoman that she was an expert on shopping and demanded to know if she should buy said pants in a small or medium, given the shrinkage-in-wash factor.

"She was nuts," the Beverly Hills saleswoman reported a year later. "I tried to be nice and told her that the pants wouldn't shrink and that she should buy the small. My luck, no more smalls were available in the Beverly Hills store. I was about to tell her that all I had to do was call the other Barneys stores and find it in a small, but then that crazy woman went ballistic, going on and on about how her life was a failure and her boyfriend had just dumped her and she lost her job and all she wanted was those pants to make her feel better."

A rumor had circulated through the store that the blond woman in question had only that morning donated a wardrobe full of halter tops, cigarette pants, and other provocative items of clothing to the Salvation Army. This rumor was backed up by a volunteer working at the organization stating, "Yeah, that lady came by and just kept dumping stuff, then she'd go back to her car and get more stuff and dump it on me. I mean, I know we're the Salvation Army and all, but what are we going to do with all these halter tops?"

In an effort to keep the peace that Barneys was known for, the saleswoman called the New York store, found the Juicy Couture pants in a small, and handed the miserable blond woman a tissue, assuring her that she would have them as soon as they came in.

"So then she was all, '*Which day?*' the Beverly Hills saleswoman continued. "I didn't know which day. How am I supposed to know? Do you see anything about me that says 'postal worker'? So I went over to my manager, who had already heard that woman screaming, and my manager said, 'Have them FedExed to the woman's house so we can get that deranged lunatic out of the store and be done with her already.' So then the miserable blond lady left, running down the stairs toward the ground floor, shouting out to me and my manager, 'I bought a four-thousand-dollar Vera Wang couture gown here once! You people should have a little more respect!' "

The miserable woman, who had only recently become one of the casualties of the Internet crash of 2001, decided to sleep in the next morning, as she forgot there was anything worth waking up for. At noon, the woman opened her apartment door to find a "While You Were Out" slip from Federal Express. Seeing no reason to continue with the day, with the exception of several trips to her kitchen to retrieve the Sara Lee pound cake and SpaghettiOs she ate at various times throughout the day and night, the woman headed back under the covers of her bed and stayed there until the following morning.

After dawn's "early" light awoke the slumbering, gloomy woman at 11:30 the next morning, she went to retrieve some leftover SpaghettiOs. Her doorbell rang.

"Who is it?" She sniveled in her crumbling state.

"FedEx," the male voice answered.

Dressed in only a tank top and Gilligan & O'Malley underwear from Target, the woman signed for her package and shut the door without saying thank you.

She opened up the package to find Juicy Couture black linen drawstring pants in a size small. After putting them on, the woman barely took them off for a year.

"I offered to buy her another pair when she came to my birthday party. I thought they looked cute on her," said a woman who identified herself as Felicia, a friend of the downhearted woman.

"I didn't think it was right for her to wear them to the job interview I got her," added Susan, another friend of the despondent woman. "And while we're on the subject, six-inch heels with Juicy Couture black linen drawstring pants are not appropriate to wear under any circumstances, especially a job interview!"

Yet it was reported that everywhere the saddened woman went, the pants were sure to follow. From cashing her unemployment check to Wednesday movie matinees with fellow ex-Internet employees, the black linen drawstring pants became a source of comfort after agonizing job interviews and deplorable dates that never went anywhere. Frequently paired with a Calvin Klein white ribbed tank top that the pants affectionately called "Tanky," the duo soon began to enjoy their newfound grimy life. They enjoyed getting up each morning/afternoon and relished experiencing where that day would take them. Most times, it didn't take them anywhere, but anything was better than sitting in that bare closet, hung on a hanger attached to a concave pole, which was rumored to have gotten that way from the weight of the piles of clothing the woman had donated to the Salvation Army several months before.

Three months into Black Linen Drawstring Pants's life, the first in a series of tragedies struck. While attending the 2001 NBA Finals basketball game between the Philadelphia 76ers and the Los Angeles Lakers at L.A.'s Staples Center, the depressed blond woman had a moment of glee and she shouted in exhilaration as Allen Iverson led the 76ers to a 107–101 win in overtime.

"Suckers!" the woman angrily shouted to the crowd of yellow-and-purple-wearing Laker fans around her.

As the crowd began to hiss and jeer and throw various junk food wrappers and half-filled cups of beer, the woman suddenly became frightened and leaped out of her seat to escape from the stadium, catching Black Linen Drawstring Pants on the armrest of

160

her seat and creating a tear on the side of the pants. The next day, the woman took the pants to her dry cleaner's, who quickly sewed up the hole and insisted on dry-cleaning the pants for free to compensate for of all the business the woman had given them the previous year.

The second in the series of tragedies occurred when the woman went to throw some trash away on a rainy night and accidentally left her keys inside. As she waited for her friend Heidi to come with her spare keys, the woman stayed at her neighbor's apartment, along with the neighbor's cat, Friskers. As the blond woman innocently tried to pet the feline, Friskers became alarmed by the rainwater dripping off the woman's body, so he opened his paw and dug his nails into Black Linen Drawstring Pants, which prompted another trip to the dry cleaner's to patch up the frayed hole they had suffered in the ghastly incident.

A week after returning home from their second stay at the dry cleaner's, Black Linen Drawstring Pants were awoken from their closet at 4 a.m. and worn for a trip back to Philadelphia.

The woman cried into her parents' arms, sobbing, "I'm a failure, I'm a failure," which her parents heartily denied.

"You're going through a rough patch," her father said. "Everything will work out, I promise."

"But those pants," her mother said, "those pants have got to go."

The saddened blond woman took their words to heart and headed back on a plane toward Los Angeles. Three days later, she was hired by the Promo House, an entertainment company, to write promotional ads for upcoming television shows.

The woman entered her apartment that evening and grabbed Black Linen Drawstring Pants. She began to put them on when, sadly, tragedy struck for the last time.

As she pulled the drawstring together, the string could no longer take the pressure and broke in two.

The woman, now in high spirits and feeling as if her life might be back on track, took off Black Linen Drawstring Pants and sighed.

As she threw the pants into the trash can, she said these final words in memoriam:

"Thank you, dear Pants for your comfort, your reassurance, your durability, and your strength, which got me through a difficult year in my life. As you continue on to that big department store in the sky, may you find the peace and joy you so deserve. I will miss you, my friend, and I promise to think of you often."

To quote W. B. Yeats's "When You Are Old"

> *And bending down beside the glowing bars;*
> *Murmur, a little sadly, how love fled*
> *And paced upon the mountains overhead*
> *And hid his face amid a crowd of stars.*

RIP:
JUICY COUTURE DRAWSTRING LINEN PANTS
2001–2002

24

Twenty-four-year-old women rock!

I'm not supposed to use the phrase "rock," though, my twenty-four-year-old work friend Kristen told me. Evidently, that's very out. Since I became friends with my young office buddies at the Promo House, I'm constantly reminded of new sayings that are in and sayings that are out.

"Rock!"

Out.

"That is off the hook!"

Out with a major cringe look.

"Bling-Bling."

Set up a firing squad.

The whole thing makes me feel out of it in a dumb, cute way, but pathetic at the same time, since I'm ten years older than these people. It's not that I'd become some old fogey in my thirties, but when you start working with people who are ten years younger than you, it can sure make you feel that way.

On my first day working at the Promo House in 2002, I wore a pair of black rayon pants and a white V-neck cotton sweater that I got on sale at the Gap. Being an office dweller for so many years, I knew not to buy anything new before I started working, because you just don't know what the style of the office is. When I arrived at the Promo House on my first day and took a look around, it was clear to me that I was overdressed and possibly overaged. The most spiffed-up woman I saw was one of the twenty-four-year-olds, wearing a Juicy Couture terry cloth sweatsuit that actually matched, both top and bottom, in baby blue. Flip-flops were the choice shoe among the who's who at the Promo House, but they loved my six-inch heels and often asked to try them on. Watching this parade of hip and trendy fashion, all I could think of was my stupidity in donating all my cool, sexy clothes because a Democrat in Republican's clothing had caught me in a yearlong lie. These girls would have loved that wardrobe. Why did I feel that I needed to punish myself so severely?

With the exception of my BFFATO (best friends forever at the office), Paula and Julian, and me—the three senior executives at the Promo House—every other person who worked there was twenty-four years old. And with the exception of my wardrobe, they all looked up to me, which I loved and, as it so happened, I looked up to them. Most were women and not girls, incredibly sweet women who were as ambitious and full of energy as they were trendy. I loved it when they asked my opinion on where I thought they should take their careers, or my advice in dealing with a new boyfriend.

Of the twenty-five people who worked there, it seemed like someone had a birthday every other day and they were always twenty-four. Even when the year passed, and we celebrated another year gone by, yet again, that person was turning twenty-four. Sometimes when I'd see the twenty-four-year-olds walk in wearing knee-high boots with short skirts, frilly tops, matching earrings, and bracelets, I wondered if it was a place for producing promo spots for television, radio, and print, or an MTV Spring Break Special. It also made me want to return to an old stomping ground I'd wondered why I'd given up on—Urban Outfitters—but it only made me feel older when I tried on the stuff and felt like one of those mothers who wears her daughter's clothes to make them look cooler. Those mothers weren't fooling anyone and, even from the dressing-room mirror, I could tell, neither was I. I opted for the alternative Urban Outfitters, the newfound Urban Outfitters of my generation, the VH1 Spring Break Special of Urban Outfitters if you will: Anthropologie.

"No, sweetheart, you tie it like *this*," HeidiAnn (no hyphen, no space), the twenty-four-year-old assistant showed me as she wrapped a scarf around my neck. It took four more wearings before I got the knot down. When I wore a new T-shirt, HeidiAnn, who had previously been to school for clothing design, took the opportunity before a meeting with a hip music channel to cut my new T-shirt into a halter top, accentuating my better body parts with diamond-shaped holes and covering up the worse ones with extra fabric. She was like Picasso with those scissors, and when I showed it to the five women you meet in Los Angeles, each gave me a T-shirt and their measurements to take to the office. HeidiAnn made $250 from my clique for her good work.

Each time I bought something that I thought was hip and with-it, it was already out of style by the time I got to the office. These twenty-four-year-olds knew their trends, and I came to rely on it. They wore designer jeans that were so in, I hadn't even heard of them.

"They're called Seven for All Mankind," Jenn with two n's

explained. "See, it's spelled out," she said, showing me the tag on the back of her jeans.

"Paper Denim & Cloth," Kristin explained as she mouthed the words slowly and as loud as she could, as if I were hard of hearing given my age. "See how it's lighter on the top and darker on the bottom? That's so the ass doesn't look as big."

I had no idea that three-quarter-length coats were so 2002 and velvet cropped jackets were the here and now. A constant question that lurked in my brain as I saw these young women arrive at work in the morning with silk babydoll T-shirts and bell-bottom jeans was, "Where did these girls get these great clothes? Had they heard about the halter-top surplus at the Salvation Army?" I could have sworn one of them was wearing an old outfit of mine.

I chose to confide in my co-thirtysomethings, Julian and Paula.

"Oh my God," Julian whispered in his distinct, excitable tone. "Isn't it crazy? It's all I ever think about. I spend more time thinking about what I'm going to wear to work than what I'm going to wear out with my boyfriend."

"I had to stop breast-feeding and put Matty on Similac," Paula admitted. "It was taking too long to pump in the morning, and I needed to spend that time finding something to wear!"

We all agreed that the tipping point of the office was Kelsey, a twenty-four-year-old junior executive who set the Promo House barometer on appearance and presentation. From her Marc Jacobs dresses to her Joie skirts, Kelsey's daily outfit was a sight that Paris couture should have taken note of. She was not to be missed, and she knew it. Kelsey was the only twenty-four-year-old I found to be difficult to get along with. Even though she was ten years younger than me, she had that edge of slickness that just screamed "most popular girl in her class," and even though I was her superior, I felt inferior to her and spoke to her as little as I had to. Her blond hair never had roots or a single split end in it.

"She must get a touchup every week!" Julian concluded.

"She must bathe it in mayonnaise," Paula added. "How else can you get that shine?"

She was by far the head of the twenty-four-year-olds; all you needed to do was hear what they said about her behind her back to know she was envied. Since the girls had made me an honorary twenty-four-year-old, it was only right that I felt the same way.

"I heard Kelsey shoplifts from Saks," Breva whispered, coming into my office one day.

"So *that's* why she's got such nice clothes!"

"I know, *RIGHT*?" she exclaimed. "And I also heard she sells coke to pay for the ones she doesn't steal."

"That is so low-rent!" I quietly roared.

"Oooh," Breva said as if she'd bit into a lemon, " 'low-rent' is a phrase from like twenty years ago."

Just then, Kelsey walked into my office, hysterically laughing while flipping her blond tresses. Breva and I braced ourselves in fear that she might have been listening.

"So wait," she said, laughing as she entered my office, "Julian just told me you donated a closet full of halter tops because a guy dumped you? Are you an idiot or something?"

I looked at Breva for any kind of help, and when I saw she wasn't going to give any, I gave Kelsey the best answer I could.

"Yes, evidently I am."

The thing I admired most about the twenty-four-year-olds was their ability to disregard any body-image issues. I could not understand how Breva, for example, all 5'1" and 160 pounds of her, could have mistaken the rolls of flab and back fat sticking out of the back of her pants for a sexy detail. The thing was, none of the other twenty-four-year-olds ever mentioned it—only Julian,

Paula, and me within the confines of our own thirtysomething alcove of talk, and none of us would ever let the twenty-four-year-olds know. The ability to show flabby flesh, we all agreed, was truly admirable. If I could have written out the conversations the five women you meet in Los Angeles and I discussed about the little piece of flesh on one's stomach or the way the top of one's thighs stuck together, it could fill volumes. The twenty-four-year-olds had no problem with it, however, and I wished I had the guts they did. If it was a generational thing and not just a Promo House thing, God bless evolution.

There was only one time that I ever disagreed with the twenty-four-year-olds.

We were all sitting in the conference room sharing a pizza when Kelsey started the debate.

"I just hate Madonna," Kelsey said. "She is so fake and I hate everything she wears."

"She is a fashion icon," I said as I cocked my newsboy hat, just like the one I'd seen her wear in *People* magazine the week before.

"Ugh," Kelsey said as she stuck her tongue out. "Now Britney," she said, "Britney could do no wrong in my book."

"She is so trashy!" I replied. "Her clothes are too small for her and her hair is so dried out. With all that money, couldn't she at least afford conditioning treatments?"

"That's her style!" Breva retorted as she pulled her T-shirt down to just above her love handles. "Britney doesn't care what anyone thinks about her. Madonna is all about what people think. She does everything for show."

"Madonna dressed a generation!" My co-thirtysomething BFFATO Paula announced as she straightened her red string Kabbalah bracelet that she got at Kitson for $40.

"Britney made it OK for us to express ourselves any way we want!" HeidiAnn shot in.

The debate went on for another couple of minutes until I excused myself from the room. There was no point in going on.

We were two generations who would never understand what it was that made the other want to emulate these women who taught us it was all right to be who we wanted to be, no matter what anyone else thought. That was the deciding difference—the rigid, inflexible conviction that would never change.

Please Excuse My Absence Today, As I Have Nothing to Wear

7:30 A.M. I've gotten out of bed an hour early this morning to shower, curl my hair, and pick out just the right outfit for my meeting with the network to pitch Promo House's ideas to be the promo writers for their new talk show. I worked all through the night with Julian, preparing our PowerPoint presentation, and we know we can do no wrong. The job is in the bag. All I have to do is look presentable, and the three hours I've given myself should do the trick. My feeling is, if I feel good, then I'll pitch good.

7:40 A.M. I'm in the shower, mentally going through my wardrobe choices. Al Roker said it's going to be "a hot one" in Southern California today. I'd like to go sleeveless since I have that Trina Turk white silk ruffled shirt that looks so cute with my black silk pants. I don't know, though. Black and white? Is that too bland?

7:58 A.M. I have to take a break and get some breakfast. Fuel up for the meeting. Fuel up for the looking in the closet. I'm thinking maybe I'll try the ruffled shirt with jeans and my faux Chanel blazer jacket. There is that heat problem though.

8:14 A.M. I look too pale for the Trina Turk white ruffled shirt, so the blazer won't even be tried on. The jeans are a bad idea too. They just look like I don't want the job, and I really want this job.

8:27 A.M. Why didn't I fake tan last night? The flowered A-line skirt I got at Anthropologie would be so perfect if I had only fake tanned. God, I'm pale.

8:45 A.M. All right, calm down. You've still got an hour and a half before the meeting. I wish I could wear my olive green Alice + Olivia corduroy pants with my black boots. Al Roker, I ask you, why "a hot one"? Why?

8:52 A.M. What about this black T-shirt with these cropped paisley pants I bought with my mother in Philadelphia that I've never worn? Is paisley in? Is paisley ever in? Do these pants look like drapes? What was I thinking, buying paisley pants? Maybe this white T-shirt would look better. Where are all my white bras? Could I pull off a black bra underneath a white T-shirt look? Is that sexy? On some people it looks cute. Whatever it is, it's not the look I want for a pitch meeting. I'm throwing these paisley pants in the trash.

9:05 A.M. Where did I get so many pairs of cropped pants? I have one, two, three, four . . . seven pairs of cropped pants! I hate cropped pants! I've got to get some regular-length pants. I should have known that cropped pants were going out when they started referring to them as "clam diggers." Rule number one: Never buy the same length pants two seasons in a row when they refer to them as something else. Maybe I'll wear a wife beater underneath the faux Chanel jacket. Note to self: Start a campaign to change the name of ribbed white shirts, aka wife beaters, to something more appealing like "the never-fail," or just "the ribbed white tank top."

9:17 A.M. OK, I'm going to look through this closet piece by piece, one more time. I'm sure I've missed something. Why do I still keep this InWear/Matinique black button-down vest? How old is this vest already? I think I got it ten, twelve years ago? Is that company still in business? Maybe I'll wear the vest with a T-shirt underneath.

9:23 A.M. I'm throwing this old vest in the trash.

9:32 A.M. I'm naked except for Target underwear, sitting on my bed and staring at my closet. Why is this so hard? Why do I have to go through this? I can't go to the pitch meeting. I'm calling in sick.

9:42 A.M. Are people wearing long skirts these days? I think I saw Gwyneth wearing one in *People* last week. OK, I'll wear this long pink skirt . . . with what shoes? With what shirt? Forget the long skirt. Why don't I have prearranged outfits? I should have outfits for occasions like pitch meetings. This is something I should have taken care of. This is why I don't have children or a husband. I'm thirty-three years old and I still can't even find something to wear in the morning. I'm so depressed. What am I doing with my life? I could seriously stick my head in the oven over this. *Thirty-three-year-old Promo House executive Adena Halpern took her own life this morning when she couldn't find anything to wear to work.* Paula in the office is so big with using her kid as an excuse, and everyone accepts it. What if I had a child to take care of? How could I find something to wear *and* get a child off to school? Paula is a really sucky dresser, though, now that I think of it. I guess it's because she's got that kid. I guess that's a part of that saying, "God gives us what he thinks we can handle." Therefore, the most I can handle—though, obviously not—is getting dressed in the morning. How pathetic and yet true.

10:02 A.M. "JULIAN, I WILL BE THERE IN TEN MINUTES!" The electricity must have gone off in my building! My alarm never went off; it's flashing 12:00. I will be there in ten minutes. WAIT FOR ME! I want to drive over to the network with you!" I hang up with Julian. Oh my God. I still have my towel on my head. I haven't even dried my hair yet. I'm literally going to have a nervous breakdown in another minute. I must start taking Yoga.

10:04 A.M. "Hi, Julian, it's me. Yeah . . . you know what, you head over there without me and I'll meet you there. . . . Yeah . . . I don't want us both to be late. . . . I have the presentation? Oh, I *do* have the presentation . . . yes, I'll e-mail you a copy."

10:15 A.M. The pitch meeting will have to do with a ponytail, a T-shirt, and jeans; I don't have time for this. I can't handle this anymore. I'm in the middle of a complete nervous breakdown because I don't have anything to wear to the pitch meeting. Why is my phone ringing? Who is calling me? "Oh, hi Julian. . . . What am I wearing? What are you wearing? You're wearing a suit?! I was just going to wear a T-shirt and jeans. . . . Well, I was thinking about putting on a blazer too. . . . The faux Chanel one with the fringe. Well, I could put on a nicer pair of pants. I have these paisley pants I've never worn . . . is paisley out? . . . I knew paisley was out. I wasn't sure; thanks for filling me in on that. You know what, we're wasting time. I'm just running out the door, I'll meet you over there."

10:27 A.M. OK, in exactly three minutes, you are going to be late because you have nothing to wear and you're standing in front of the closet you've already surveyed ten times this morning. You are a failure in life. You are going to get fired because you have nothing to wear. What am I going to tell my parents when I ask them to borrow money? Just pick anything! Anything! I'll go through this closet one more time, piece by piece.

10:34 A.M. I can't believe I'm wearing this ugly pink long skirt. Does this even go with this faux Chanel fringe jacket? I am so uncomfortable, where are my car keys? Oh, here they are.

10:40 A.M. Screw it; I'll just wear the jeans. No one can see my pants under the table anyway, and they'll be too busy staring at my hair and wondering why it's still wet.

10:43 A.M. Should I wear the skirt?

10:45 A.M. "Hi, Julian, it's me. . . . Oh, you're sitting in their lobby waiting to go in? Tell them my kid was sick. . . . JUST TELL THEM THAT MY CHILD WAS SICK. . . . JUST TELL THEM THAT I HAVE A CHILD! . . . I DON'T CARE IF IT'S A BOY OR A GIRL! FINE IT'S A GIRL! . . . MORGAN, MADELYN, MONICA, PICK ONE! By the way, I'm wearing jeans and my faux Chanel jacket.

10:50 A.M. "You know what? Don't tell them I have a kid, then they'll always ask me about the kid if we get the job and it will go on and on and on and oh God, the consequences. Just tell them my electricity went out. . . . YES, MY ELECTRICITY DID GO OUT. . . . NO, I'M NOT LYING! GOOD-BYE.

10:51 A.M. "Hi, it's me again. Yes, I was lying. I couldn't find anything to wear. Just tell them my car wouldn't start. By the way, could we go shopping after this pitch meeting? Great. See you in ten minutes."

Those Shoes Are Kind of High, Aren't They?

don't know how I could have gotten through life if Oprah Winfrey didn't have a television show. I can honestly say that I've barely missed a day in all the years she's been on the air. When I first started taking birth-control pills years ago, the doctor said to make sure I take them at a daily time I'm always aware of. Most people pick the time they wake up or when they go to sleep at night. I picked three in the afternoon, the time of day I'm most aware of. That's when Oprah comes on in Los Angeles. Did you know, for example, that a new bra should only go on the loosest hook? The other two behind it are for if and when the bra's elastic stretches. Fascinating, right? Learned it from Oprah. I know tons of facts like this. From the fact that cropped pants make you look shorter to the fact that Ralph Lauren makes these really great cashmere cable-knit sweaters, I am constantly bringing up facts or being reminded of tips that I learned from watching Oprah.

There was this particular *Oprah Winfrey Show* years ago where

Oprah and her guest were talking about what do to when "the guy of your dreams" is in an elevator with you. The guest advised Oprah and the audience to just "say anything," whatever it is, "Nice weather we're having," or "What time is it?" Just say anything to get a conversation rolling, or you'll always regret it. This was what was going through my head when I got into the elevator at the eighth-floor Promo House offices to get down to the first floor of the building.

He was damn fine, as the twenty-four-year-olds might say (but of course I had to ask them to make sure). Although I'd find out later that he was a staunch Democrat, he wasn't one in Republican's clothing, and he wasn't a taller-than-tall olive-skinned boy in a leather jacket. He was more than that. He had an air about him, that *Je ne sais quoi* that screamed self-assured and entitled to anything he wanted on the basis that he was him. These were my first impressions in the three seconds since I had entered the elevator. He was medium height, in his early forties, with dark brown hair and was dressed down in jeans, a black T-shirt, and black driving shoes. It was lust from that first second the elevator doors opened. As I entered the elevator, I gave him an acknowledging half-smile, turned my back to him, and pressed the Lobby button, which he had already pushed before I got in there. From the time the doors shut and the elevator started going down, Oprah Winfrey was screaming inside my head, "NICE WEATHER WE'RE HAVING! NICE WEATHER WE'RE HAVING!" I watched the floor numbers above the door light up like a countdown, 8, 7, 6, . . . and that's when I decided to make my move. I was just taking a quick deep breath and was preparing the words when he beat me to it.

"Those shoes are kind of high, aren't they?" he asked. I turned around to find him smiling with this sincere look that might have begged another question.

"I suppose so," I sort of whispered shyly. "I'm a heel freak," I explained, continuing to half-smile. I immediately turned my back to him and stared at the numbers above the door, 5, 4, 3 . . .

"Nice weather we're having," I said turning back again.

"If you like rain," he said.

"Is it raining?" I full-smiled, getting caught.

He chuckled at this.

We stood for a long second in silence as the doors opened to the lobby.

"Do you work in this building?" he asked me as we walked out of the elevator.

"Eighth Floor, the Promo House," I think I answered.

"I'm on the tenth floor; I have a company up there," he said as we continued walking. "I'm Pete Rodgers," he offered, extending his hand.

I gave him my name and shook his hand, I think.

"You're the cutest thing I've ever seen," he said with no feeling, just matter-of-fact, like this was his conclusion. He busily walked the other way, off to wherever he had to go, taking a right in the lobby as I took my left. "Drop by and say hi sometime," he called out with a big smile, but still in that same nothing-to-write-home-about tone.

As I walked through the lobby doors and into the rainy day outside, I looked at my watch, opened my bag, and took that day's birth control pill. A crush had been formed at exactly three that afternoon.

"Pete Rodgers told you that you were cute?" Jesse shouted as she typed his name into the Internet Movie Database on her computer. "You have SO GOT to go up there and say hello! Do you have any idea who he is? Take a look at his credits!" she said, showing me the screen.

The guy who thought I was the cutest thing he'd ever seen had won an Academy Award, two Golden Globes, four MTV Movie Awards, and a Blockbuster Award.

"Go up there right now," Kristen said, grabbing my purse and handing it to me. Tell him you're dropping by like he told you to," Kristen shouted, jumping up and down.

There was no way on earth I was going to do that. While I wished I was one of those types of women who could do that, I just wasn't.

"Be assertive," HeidiAnn said, stomping her feet and pulling jabs at me.

"You people are crazy," I told them. "What is he, Mae West, I'm gonna 'come up and see him sometime'?"

They looked at me cockeyed, not getting the reference.

"She was a very talented and popular comic actress from the thirties on through the sixties."

"That's all the more reason." Jesse stomped. "You know all that film stuff!"

Yes, I thought he was hot—I thought he was gorgeous—and yes, the crush deepened a little more with the thought of checking out his Academy Award. Still, I had no guts.

"You're going to regret it for the rest of your life," HeidiAnn said as the girls walked out of my office.

That Friday afternoon, I was bored out of my mind trying to come up with titles for a new dating show when it occurred to me: Why *shouldn't* I go up and say hello? What was the big deal? Like the sister I was, I was gonna "do it for myself." The twenty-four-year-olds needed to see how it was done with strength, honor, and respect. Luckily I was wearing my favorite black three-quarter-length black jersey shirt from Banana Republic and Theory capri khakis instead of my usual hot yellow terry cloth knockoff Juicy sweats I'd worn three times that week.

"Where are you going?" Jesse asked as I passed her reception desk.

"Nowhere, I just need some air."

"Some tenth-floor air?" She grinned.

"Well, yes, I thought the altitude would do me some good. You know, clear my head. I've got some writer's block right now."

"Some Academy Award–winning writer's block?" She grinned again as she winked.

"Oh, shut up already," I told her as I pressed the Up elevator button.

What happened next, I'll even admit in my own romantically desperate quasi-religious pursuit of signs, was a meant-to-be happenstance that Jesse would tell over and over and over to anyone in the office who would listen. And far be it from me, I was not going to stop her.

"Hi!" he said as the elevator doors opened and we locked eyes.

"Oh, hi!" I answered back, obviously surprised.

He got off of the elevator and onto my floor.

"Were you going somewhere?"

"I was going to get some air."

"I was just coming down to say hello to you. Would it be all right if I got some air with you?"

"I'm sure there's enough to go around," I said with a smile.

"Great," Pete said, catching the elevator door as it was about to close again.

I looked over at Jesse as I turned to walk in. She was mouthing the words *"Oh my God,"* as she gave me a thumbs-up sign.

"I just don't see how you can walk in those," he managed to say at the exact moment I lightly tripped over a doormat in the lobby.

"I don't know how to walk otherwise," I joked. "Take off my shoes, and my feet are permanently locked at a ninety-degree angle."

"Do you hate your height?" he asked as we took a seat at the coffee place next to the building.

"Yes," I admitted, "I hate my height."

"How tall are you? Five three?"

"Yeah, about that." I wished.

"I don't understand why women want to be taller. I love petite women. I love how they're just so dainty and fragile-looking." He took a look under the table again. "I mean, you could kill some-one with those heels."

"Who says I haven't?" I said flirtatiously.

"Who did you kill?" he asked seriously, as if I'd gotten out of jail and the probation board got me a job at the Promo House.

"The last guy who harped on my shoes."

"Enough said," he concluded as he walked up to order our coffees. "She'll have a mocha latte," he ordered without asking me, "grande, like her heels."

That made me laugh.

We left our office building together an hour later and spent the entire weekend at his beach house in Malibu. The only clothing we ever wore was our underwear, me in Target underwear, him in saggy tighty whities. A match made in 100% cotton heaven.

As the elevator reached the eighth floor that Monday morn-ing, the same high heels, khaki pants, and three-quarter-length black jersey shirt from Banana Republic stepped out to face another workweek. The blond-haired girl kissed her new Block-buster Award–winning boyfriend and sent him on up to his tenth-floor space. As she walked into the reception area, greeting her dear receptionist friend Jesse with a warm hug, she went back to her office, ignoring Jesse's cries for information, shut the door, and sighed happily at her computer. The cursor was still blinking at the same spot she'd left it at on Friday. She stared at the cursor for the rest of the morning with a deep, dreamy gaze until a mes-senger entered her office with a package at one that afternoon. It was a pair of pink ballet flats. The card was signed *"So it will be that much more difficult for you to get rid of me, with love, P."*

Send Me the Bill

"Have you thought about what you're going to wear to my premiere?" Pete asked one morning, six months into our relationship. I was standing in my closet, searching for a suitable outfit for the Promo House's weekly Tuesday-morning office meeting.

"Serena and I are going to start the search on Friday," I brushed off as I contemplated my red corduroy pants from Abercrombie & Fitch versus a BCBG flouncey beige skirt.

"How would you like to have a stylist pick something out for you?"

The question stopped me in my decision-making process. It wasn't like I hadn't spent silent hours deep in the middle of the night while Pete was sleeping with thoughts about exactly what I wanted to wear for his movie premiere. Serena and I had already had preliminary discussions over it. Previous movie premiere segments from *Access Hollywood* and *Entertainment Tonight* had been

TiVoed for research. To pay someone else to go through that pain and torture for me could only feel like shopping's morphine drip. Yes, I could get addicted to something like that.

"So, what would the stylist do?" I asked him like I didn't know. Truthfully, I wasn't sure of the whole process.

"She'd grab a whole bunch of stuff for you. I'd like to see you in a dress; you don't show off your legs enough," he said, leaning over the bed and caressing my calf.

"Someone else told me that once," I said, looking down at the gams, "but what about, like, accessories and that kind of thing?"

"She gets you all that stuff. Shoes, jewelry, anything you need. I already asked Lina, this stylist I know who's done stuff for me in the past, if she wouldn't mind working with you."

I had already thought of him as the most wonderful boyfriend on the planet, but this, this kicked him up to the stratosphere.

"So how many outfits does she come up with?" I asked, sitting back on the bed, mostly for cushioning in case I fainted from the exhilaration.

"A bunch." He smiled, knowing that had I been connected to an EKG, the thing would have been beeping off the chart.

"And then I just pick one out? What if I don't like anything she brings?" I asked in sheer delight.

"She goes out and finds more stuff!" he said outwardly looking so fulfilled, since he knew he was offering me my version of the Hope Diamond.

My smile said it all. I suddenly knew how Charlie felt, being offered Wonka's factory.

"Will it be expensive?" I asked.

"Send me the bill."

"No," I said, getting up. "Forget it. I can't have you buying me expensive outfits like that. It wouldn't feel right. I'd feel like one of those women."

"What women?"

"The ones with the breast implants and perfect bodies that Los Angeles is known for."

"Don't worry. You could not be further from being one of those women," he said, taking me into his arms.

"I can't decide if that's a compliment or not."

"You take it as you're nothing like those kinds of women, or any woman. You are one-of-a-kind."

"You are good," I said with a laugh.

"No, seriously," he whispered as he looked into my eyes. "You really are one-of-a-kind, and this is something I want to do for you. Let me do it."

"I don't know if this is the right time to say this," I said, nuzzling my head into his neck, "but I think I'm, like, in love with you."

He kissed me on the forehead. "If I knew that getting you a stylist was going to make you fall in love with me, I would have gotten you one six months ago."

We kissed passionately as he added, "Because that's when I fell in love with you."

I could have died happy then and there. Had a bus come plowing into the bedroom and killed me, it would have been absolutely fine. I had a man who loved me, peace of mind, and, above all else, a stylist who would make me look amazing in that casket.

The Holy Land

I'm just going to admit it.

Having a stylist come to your house with the perfect Prada black empire-waist dress is a euphoria that the depths of imagination just cannot duplicate.

You might have thought that the Five women were waiting for Jesus to resurrect himself at my door, and it was getting on my last nerve.

"You're making more of this than it needs to be!" I screamed at Heidi as she put the carefully decorated tray of crudités along with three kinds of dip on my coffee table.

"Who knows how long we're going to be here," she said as the other four dug in.

My mother called from Philadelphia.

"Is she there yet?" she asked Felicia, who had picked up the phone.

"No," Felicia announced, "we're still waiting."

"Put me on the speaker phone," Arlene told her. "I don't want to miss a second. I'm there in spirit girls!" my mother shouted.

"MOTHER, PLEASE!" I shouted back at her. "Why is everyone making such a big deal out of this? It's not my wedding, you know!"

"I pray to God, if it could only be," Arlene implored.

"I think our girl is nervous," Felicia told everyone present and the one in absentia. "She's giving that cranky tone."

"OUT!" I shouted. "ALL OF YOU, OUT! MOTHER, GOOD-BYE!"

Just as I said that, the doorbell rang. We all went silent.

"Get the door," I instructed Rachel.

"Should I?" Rachel pondered as she looked at Heidi, who looked at Serena, who took a carrot and dipped it into some sun-dried tomato dip. Felicia handed her a napkin.

"Well, *I'm* not going to get it," my mother announced.

"Hello!" the voice from outside shouted. "Is anyone there?"

"My God!" Susan grumbled, walking swiftly to grab the door. "There are women in the world who couldn't care less about something like this."

Susan ran over to the door and opened it, and a heap of wardrobe bags came toward her with a violent thrust, sending Susan's long black curls hurling backward. Behind the bags was Lina the stylist.

"I just have to grab the shoes," Lina said, disappearing from the door as quickly as she came.

The Five and I dragged the garment bags into the house and into my bedroom.

"What's happening?" my mother inquired over the speaker phone.

"Nothing yet," Serena informed her. "We're taking the clothes back into the bedroom."

"And here's the last batch," Lina said, getting to work and entering my bedroom with stacks of shoes.

"All those shoes?" Rachel gasped. "How are we going to decide?"

"How many shoes?" my mother asked.

"What is that?" Lina sourly inquired.

"I'm the mother," Arlene introduced herself from the speaker phone.

"Pleased to meet you," Lina answered as she gave me a quizzical look.

"She likes to be a part of things like this," I embarrassingly admitted, watching Lina zip open the first garment bag.

"Pete mentioned that he wanted you in a dress," she said, ignoring my explanation and taking a once-over of my body. "Now that I look at your figure," she continued, taking her hands and putting them on my waist, "I think the Vivienne Westwood would sit nicely around your torso." She circled me like a shark. "Oh, wait . . . no, forget the Westwood; you have no ass and the dress will hang in the back."

"It's the curse of our family," Arlene confessed from the speaker. "None of the women in my family have a backside."

Lina continued circling me, the Five watching Lina watching me as she examined my body. She threw her hair on top of her head, took a pen from her purse, and stuck it in the bun she'd created to make a stylish up-do. Then she threw her hands on her hips and let out a huge sigh.

"OK, the good news is that you have nice shoulders. The bad news is that everything else has to be pushed up and pulled in. We're going to need a girdle for your stomach, the bust gets a padded push-up bra, we'll use a shaper for those thighs, and of course we need some pads for that flat ass. By the way, Pete said you were five three, I don't think you're five three."

"She's five two and a half," Susan defended, putting her arm around me quite possibly to control me from grabbing the metal spreader from the ranch-dressing dish on the crudités tray in order to stab myself in my girdle-required flab of a stomach.

It was becoming clear to me as to why all those Los Angeles women Pete and I mentioned got boob jobs and worked out incessantly to achieve perfect bodies. Stylists like Lina tore them from flabby limb to floppy chin.

"Trust me though," she said, "you've got a much better body than a lot of actresses I've worked with." She mouthed the names of some A-list actresses.

"No!" we gasped as Lina ballooned her cheeks when mentioning the blond siren with the enormous thighs.

"I was wondering what the deal was with those turtlenecks!" We all shouted, laughing when Lina mentioned the goiter problem on *Vanity Fair*'s pick of Hollywood's latest American sweetheart.

"I can't hear! Who'd she say?" my mother begged.

The Vivienne Westwood white dress with accents of gold-encrusted flowers and a bustled back went on first.

"Oh, that's awful," Heidi agreed, circling me along with Lina. "Her ass is way too flat in that."

"Don't worry, Dean. It's a common thing," Felicia said. "Lots of women have no asses."

"It's so funny," Lina remarked. "Pete's ex-wife had a flat ass too."

"So I guess guys do make passes at girls with flat asses," Susan joked.

"Next!" Serena commanded.

I threw on the John Galliano bloodred pouf skirt as Lina cinched the bustier top, throwing me back to prom night.

"Absolutely not," Arlene shouted from the phone as Heidi described the dress. "How's she going to sit in the seat?"

"Good point," I said, grabbing another dress.

The vintage Carolina Herrera black strapless cocktail dress was too snug.

"Renée felt the same way," Lina divulged as I turned to Serena, who mouthed, *"Zellweger."*

"She was still at her Bridget Jones weight," Lina said, handing me the Stella McCartney.

"You want to be in Stella," Lina sharply advised, "so pray that this fits. Stella is so environmentally friendly," she explained. "And that is so in right now."

Unfortunately, the rust-colored corset wasn't friendly to my environment.

"Oh God no, take it off! Take it off!" the girls shouted in unison.

According to Heidi, the Calvin Klein mini A-line shift in white just didn't feel right.

"It's just not . . . you. I don't feel your personality shining through," she said, visibly searching for words.

The Marc Jacobs 1950s-inspired pencil skirt didn't sit right, according to Felicia.

"It's too sophisticated," she said.

The Donna Karan tuxedo jacket made me look like an *Annie Hall* reject, according to Susan.

"La de da, la de da, la take it off," she said, waving her arms.

The Ralph Lauren asymmetrical silk charmeuse floor-length in midnight blue was simply not made with my body type in mind, Lina concluded.

"It's Claudia, Elle, Cindy, and Kate, but no offense, not you."

Rachel felt that the printed chiffon Anna Sui would have been more suited for daytime.

My mother had to take another phone call, but disagreed with Rachel before hanging up, and Rachel took back her statement and said, "And then again, it could be for nighttime too."

The Catherine Malandrino pleated leather skirt did nothing for my calves, according to Heidi.

"It's the cut of it or something; it just knocks your calves in half."

An hour into our fashion show, Pete showed up in a yellow T-shirt and red pants.

"Are you working part-time at McDonald's now or something?" Susan joked.

"I'm not the fashion plate," he said, kissing me on the cheek and looking over all the clothes. "Hey, let's see that black dress," he casually remarked.

I put on the Prada empire-waist chiffon strapless.

"It's perfect," Pete said, surveying the last of the crudités on the tray.

"I like it," Susan said.

"Yeah, that's the one," Heidi said.

"She's a dream in it," Felicia contentedly responded.

"It just looks like it says *premiere*." Serena sighed, sitting back on my bed.

"If you all say it's right, I think so too," Rachel concluded.

"Great," Pete said. "Anyone want to order a pizza?"

And that completed one of the greatest shopping experiences of my life.

Girdles, Corsets, and Other Ways of Killing Yourself

want to know who the jerk was who decided that bulbous was unpopular.

What's wrong with a little girth hanging out of one's dress? What is so horrible about some extra padding in the derriere region? Somewhere along the way, the guys (and no doubt they were guys) at the girdle company got together with the guys at the corset company and said, "Hey, I know how we can take advantage of women's insecurities for the next couple of centuries. . . ."

Wouldn't it be wonderful to dream that one day we all got the notion that breasts got more attractive the lower they got? To think of the day when the pear-shape body would be the body to try to achieve, and microminiskirts would be the norm to show off our cellulite with sex appeal and merriment?

Next week, my boyfriend and I are going to the first big gala premiere of the year and here's what I'm wearing: I'll be in a bra that makes my breasts look bigger, a body shaper to make my stomach look smaller, six-inch stilettos to make me appear taller, and I'm covering it all up with a black dress that, as Lina the stylist put it, "makes you look so thin, you disappear when you turn sideways." Do I really want to look so thin that I vanish?

Uh, yeah.

Whether we like it or not, we live in the unfortunate age where you can never be too thin. No matter how much we American women try to tell one another that the average size is a size ten, there's always going to be some wiry broad in the store on the verge of tears because she has to get the pants in a size four when she's always been a size two.

Heidi's cousin Nancy has the most perfect body of anyone I know. When she gave birth to her daughter last year, she was like someone in the movies who had the baby and all of a sudden her belly instantly went back to the way it was before she was pregnant. Still, Nancy complained that she had "excess skin" around her stomach. She and Heidi were both asked to be bridesmaids at Heidi's brother's wedding the following month, and Nancy was steadfast in getting rid of that extra skin. Every time I spoke to Nancy for the next few weeks, she was in the middle of doing crunches.

The night of the wedding, Nancy looked ravishing. Friends were coming up to her in droves, unable to believe she'd just had a baby. As Heidi and Nancy were standing next to the bride and groom, I saw Nancy tap Heidi on the back. Later, Heidi told me what happened.

"I'm going to die," Nancy whispered to her.

"Why?" Heidi whispered back.

"I've been stabbed. You've got to help me. I've got to get out of here."

Heidi looked around the room to see if anyone might notice the bride's only two bridesmaids leaving the scene of the *chuppa*.

"Wait two seconds," Heidi said. "We'll run out as soon as it's over."

"No," Nancy said, "I can't take it."

With that, Nancy stopped the Rabbi in midsentence and excused herself from the platform.

The room went buzzing.

Turned out, a wire on the corset that Nancy was wearing had broken and had stabbed her in the ribs. She was even bleeding. A doctor had to be called in and she had to be given a tetanus shot. Heidi's brother, of course, berated Nancy afterward, telling her she'd single-handedly ruined his wedding.

After that, Nancy decided that she would never again wear anything that would constrict her body for the sake of fashion. Even if she had ten more babies, no matter what happened to her body, she would always go sans corset or girdle top. When I heard this, I wanted to boost her up and put her on a pedestal for all the good she was showing the women of the world. I only wished that I'd had the guts that Nancy had.

A week later, Nancy called Heidi from the hospital. She'd just had some lipo done and needed a ride home.

Who Are You Wearing?

f you've never been to a movie premiere where your hot boyfriend produced the movie, I'm telling you now: It's awesome. It's enough to know that you get all the soda and popcorn your teeth would want to decay for, but even better, walking that red carpet hand-in-hand with your gorgeous boyfriend in a black Prada suit with a white shirt and a black tie and you wearing a black Prada dress with an empire waist that Lina the stylist picked out for you for the occasion is an experience unparalleled. Hundreds of flashbulbs blind you as you try to act as calm as you possibly can; stand as straight as you possibly can; and smile bright, though not too bright (like you secretly practiced in the mirror before the event); while photographers scream your name, albeit wrong—"Deanna!" "Adonna!" "Deandra!" But who cares? It makes you feel like you've cured cancer.

I couldn't help but feel a little short in the Christian Louboutin heels, though.

"You're, like, nine feet tall in them," Pete said, looking down at me. "Those other shoes you wear are too high anyway."

He could have been right, but even as I was enjoying the attention I was getting for dating the famous producer, it was something that irked in my brain.

Walking down that red carpet, stopping at every step for Pete to be interviewed and photographed, I loved how he held my hand as I prayed that anyone from Harriton High School's 1987 graduating class would be watching *Access Hollywood* the following night when the interviewer said to him, "And who's this gorgeous lady on your arm?" followed by Pete's perfectly enunciated, self-assured, indisputable response of "The gorgeous lady on my arm is my girlfriend Adena Halpern," followed by the interviewer turning the mic to me and asking, "Adena, who are you wearing tonight?" Followed by my efficient and sophisticated toned answer, "We're both in Prada tonight." What a feeling! Much to my great sorrow, however, that part didn't make it on *Access Hollywood*, but if anyone was watching that night and didn't blink, they would have seen me in a very brief shot giving an air-kiss hello to the actress who starred in the movie.

There's something about wearing a $3,000 dress that makes you stand up straighter, smile brighter, feel thinner. Sure, I had about twenty yards of Lycra underneath the dress, pulling in my thighs and stomach and blooming my size 32A breasts, making them look like I could nurse Wisconsin. Still, the feeling of walking into the ladies' room and turning around to get a look at my padded ass silhouetted by the black Prada over it was a feeling I'd never felt before. Everything looked like I wanted it to. The boobs were up and cleavaged. The stomach was in. The ass was . . . I had an ass! Everything was where it was supposed to be, and like Narcissus before me, I might have missed the rest of the party altogether because I could not get over my own reflection in the mirror.

"That's a great dress," I heard as I turned to see a blond-haired woman in a white Versace suit standing before me. "You look great in it. It's Prada, right?"

I nodded, affirming her question. I think.

"I'll have to call over for that," she said, straightening her red string Kabbalah bracelet and walking out the door like a ray of light as quickly as she walked in.

"Was that who I think it was?" another woman in the ladies' room asked me.

I couldn't answer her. I couldn't think. I couldn't breathe, and I'd lost all feeling in my body. I had gone blind. I stared back at the woman, trying to find clarity along with the oxygen my body was begging for.

"She's calling over for my dress!" I eeked out.

The Sixth Woman You Meet
in Los Angeles

Lina had become my new best friend, the kind who you can say anything to and vice versa, and a new member of our group.

She had also become the one to call for any situation.

"I have a baby shower in two weeks!" Serena cried.

"Masse Made to Measure on North Flores, white-and-blue-striped dress, right side of the store, fourth dress in on the third rack," Lina told her.

"Should I get the blue T-shirt or the green one, or maybe the red one?" Rachel cried.

"Green. Goes with your eyes," Lina told her.

"Emmy Awards. She wants to know if she can wear pants," Susan's assistant asked.

"Which row is she sitting in?"

"Sixteenth row."

"No. She must wear a dress. Any woman sitting in the first twenty rows wears a dress."

She was blunt (most times too blunt), savvy, extremely knowledgeable, and most of all, naturally fashionable. It is my belief that there are a few people in this world—not many, just some—who have the ability to use the side of their brain that's meant for picking out the best outfits possible for any occasion. You know that person. It could be a friend, but more possibly an enemy who arrives at the party or the restaurant or the supermarket in just the right jeans or dress and accessorized with exactly the right earrings or bracelet. This was Lina.

For Lina's personal style, however, she didn't wear Prada or Chloé or Dior. They wore her, and this was something I took early note of. Her body was nothing to scream about. She was on the tall side, about 5'6", she was naturally thin and didn't work out, leaving some flab here and there; but her attitude about the clothes on her back was that she hated everything, but wore it on the basis of the fact that she needed to put something on. This was why she looked good in them. She wasn't *excited* about the Chanel suit she borrowed from a photo shoot. What mattered was that it fit accordingly on the body and for the occasion. The gold bangled bracelets or hoop earrings that she threw on as she was running out the door might have taken me hours to contemplate. Not Lina. She was a professional.

"How do you do it?" I asked her one day when she showed up for lunch wearing a large scarf wrapped around her waist, forming a tight-fitting miniskirt and an old, worn gray T-shirt with just the right sags in the neck and tightness in the sleeves.

"It was ninety degrees today," she said, grabbing a piece of bread. "All my other skirts were in the laundry, so I had to improvise."

"And how long did it take you to do that?"

"I don't know," she said, trying to change the subject, acting like it was the most ridiculous of conversations. "Like, on the way to my car in the garage."

On the work front, I had taken Kelsey's place as the fashion plate of the Promo House and the twenty-four-year-olds were thrilled with the conquest.

"Where did you get that top?" Kelsey asked as I passed her in the hall.

"Oh this? It was sent over to me. It's Stella McCartney." I brushed off the comment. "You know, Stella is so environmentally friendly, and that's what I'm all about right now."

For the two of us, I don't know how much money Pete paid Lina. (He wouldn't tell me, saying, "Who cares, just as long as you're happy.") But she became a central figure in our house, which was something I sorely needed.

Almost every night, there was an occasion to be dressed for.

Whether it was a black-tie benefit to cure AIDS, diabetes, autism, heart disease, Alzheimer's, or breast, ovarian, prostate, or lung cancer, there was the perfect dress that went along with it.

If there was a benefit to raise awareness about rape; starving children; starving children in Africa; starving children in Chechnya, the Sudan, or Russia; suicide; women's issues; men's issues; terrorism; politics; mental health; or pollution, there was a dress that went along with it.

We were always getting dressed up to save something, whether it was the whales, the water, the rain forest, the redwood trees, the children, arctic wildlife, the black rhino, the chimps, the Pacific Northwest tree octopus, or the manatees—which I thought said "matinees" on the invite and was excited to go, since going to the movies in the afternoon has always been a passion of mine. One week, after three nights of hobnobbing to save this or that, we were at an organ-transplant-awareness dinner and Pete joked to our table as we dug into the pâté, "Save the liver" in a Julia Child/Dan Aykroyd *SNL* impersonation that no one else at our table thought was as hysterically funny as the two of us did.

And everywhere we went, someone got an award. There was the lifetime achievement award for film, television, and theatre. There were the crossover awards, the ones given to famous actors or directors who had a passion for those living in poverty, or who had just made a movie about someone who suffered from muscular dystrophy. At first, I felt it was important to lend my support to these events. After a while, however, it was like a TV movie's cliché: the disease of the week. One night, Pete got an award for his achievement in helping to bring the arts back into inner-city schools. We forgot that he was being honored until we got to the benefit and saw his picture on the marquee.

"What disorder are we honoring tonight?" I asked Pete one morning as we were brushing our teeth.

"I think it's spina bifida . . . no, it's something about getting kids off drugs."

It wasn't that we didn't care. We did; especially Pete. He was always wanting to give back for all the success he'd achieved, and I respected that and wholeheartedly read up on that particular night's event. The problem was that it was getting to the point where nothing was special anymore. I had overdosed on black tie and charity.

Still, there was Lina, arriving on the afternoon of the event with the dress for the occasion. Underwear from Target was heading farther and farther back into the lingerie drawer, being replaced by padded underwear and girdle tops. One day Pete came home with a huge box for me. I opened it to find forty pairs of Cosabella underwear.

"They were a PR thing that Cosabella sent over," he said, grabbing a banana and looking at his BlackBerry. "They want us to put it on the actress for the new movie. I told them to send some over for you. I love to see you in sexy underwear."

So I started wearing the boy-cut sheers in black, red, and pink.

My six-inch heels were being replaced by three-inch heels, which I felt way too short in until Lina assured me that my other shoes were "horrible."

"You're not fooling anyone with those high heels," she said. "Everyone can plainly see that you're four-eleven."

"Five-two and a half," I sauced back at her.

"Yes, with the three-inch heels, you're five-two and a half. It's time to be the real you," she said, putting her arms around me and making me feel like I was at some sort of an intervention. "Accept your height. Get real. Use what you have."

As I entered Serena's house for a dinner party one night she looked down at me and said, "Why do you look so short?"

"I'm being the real me," I told her as I slumped by.

I came home one day to find that all of my Calvin Klein athletic bras were gone, and push-up bras sat in their place. Cosabella sent Pete's office more than forty bras that all happened to be my size—32A. If there is one thing I know for sure in this world, lace push-up bras, while stunning to look at, are not for running on the treadmill. The support is shockingly bleak and, frankly, downright itchy from the lace. The feeling of pulling your bra down at each interval is not a milestone of celebration one wants to display on a busy Saturday at the gym.

In short, I was starting to hate Lina. I started to hate what she brought me for each occasion. I missed Banana Republic backroom sales and buying Drano, Comet, and Tide laundry detergent along with my underwear at Target.

"Never wash your clothes with low-class laundry detergent," Lina scolded me once. "Caldrea, Good Home, or Beach House. Those are the only products I would ever use."

One night, I'd just had enough.

There was a dinner honoring a woman who had learned to walk again after being crushed in an auto accident that left her paralyzed from the waist down. Lina thought this occasion called for the shortest of skirts.

"It's a celebration of the legs," she said. "It's the one thing you've both got going for you."

I almost slapped her after that statement.

I looked at Pete as I watched him put on the John Varvatos blue suit, the one that Lina and I had picked out for him the week before at the opening of the new John Varvatos shop on Melrose.

"I can't do this tonight," I told him. "I have to put on sweats and order Chinese," I said, sinking onto the bed and clutching the blankets.

"I'm glad you said that," he said, loosening his tie. "I was thinking the same thing."

He threw himself on the bed next to me and we embraced.

"I'm starting to lose brain cells from all that Lycra," I said, laughing.

"Maybe we should have a benefit for you," he joked.

"I am going to throw on my nastiest, oldest sweats and that crazy sweater you had woven from your dead dog's fur," I said, getting up.

"Don't be mean to Banjo's memory; I love that sweater." He pouted, grabbing the sweater and petting the arm. "It's like Banjo is still here."

"If you love it, I love it," I said, grabbing an old pair of sweatpants.

"Hey, put on the sweats that Lina got for you," he said in that matter-of-fact tone I'd come to know so well.

Making Scents

My aunt Judy Savitt had come to Los Angeles on vacation, and we made plans to have dinner one night. As Judy got into my car and I started to drive, I smelled a wonderful scent that to me screamed hugs, laughter, frustration, appreciation, degradation, admiration, anger, respect, disapproval, and, of course, love.

"Are you wearing Carolina Herrera perfume?" I asked her.

"Yes, how did you know?"

"It suddenly smelled like my mom was here."

It's hard for me to date a guy who wears Cartier cologne. It smells like my father is there, watching every move the guy makes.

I can be in a department store and a perfume saleswoman will ask me if I want to try Giorgio Armani's Acqua Di Gio.

"Why bother?" I tell her. "All I have to do is go to my friend

Rachel's house and smell her. Same goes for my friend Susan and Burberry Brit."

Luckily Heidi has a big mouth or I'd never know she'd entered a room; she's allergic to perfume.

Someone at the next table in a restaurant will be squeezing some lemon into her Diet Coke and I will suddenly think of Serena. She always wears this fragrance she first bought in Paris called Eau d'Hadrien by Annick Goutal. Very lemony and fresh. I get the same feeling when I take a sniff of makeup powder and automatically think of my childhood best friend Amy Chaikin's Anaïs Anaïs fetish in high school. Amy called me recently and told me that she's really into wearing Marc Jacobs perfume. Since we live three thousand miles away from each other, whenever I miss her, I take a sniff of it in a department store. It makes me feel a little closer to my dear old friend. My other childhood best friend Julie Pelagatti and I have lost touch. We had a disagreement a couple of years ago. I honestly can't remember what it was about. As teenagers, just before we'd head into a party, Julie would spritz on some Giorgio by Giorgio Beverly Hills that she kept in her glove compartment. Just last week, a woman passed me on the street wearing that unmistakably abundant bouquet of jasmine, rose, and amber. It made me very sad.

It's not so much the smell of Fragile perfume by Jean Paul Gaultier that makes me think of my cousin Michele. It's the cool snow globe with the gold flakes that fly around the pretty lady inside wearing the strapless black dress. Every time I'm in Michele's bedroom, I shake the bottle. Same goes for when I'm in a department store. It's so fun and glamorous, just like my cousin who wears it.

The smell of Calvin Klein's Obsession, however, makes me think about my taxes. It's the scent my accountant wears. Hemp hair gel's citrus scent reminds me that I have to get my teeth cleaned. It's the aroma I smell on Dr. Oche, my dentist, when he's looking into my mouth. I Profumi di Firenze smells like I have to get my roots done. It's my hairdresser's signature scent.

My signature fragrance is Donna Karan's Cashmere Mist body lotion. I like the body lotion scent better than the scent that comes from the atomizer. It just smells cleaner, less alcohol-y, I don't know. I've asked saleswomen why, and they tell me it's something in the mix of the lotion and perfume or something like that. I've also tried the Cashmere Mist shampoo, conditioner, deodorant, and decorative scented candle but, in the end, I've found that using the body lotion is just enough. Too much, and I start to feel like I could sprout a garden out of my ears. I've been wearing Cashmere Mist for years—not for everyday, but for nights that I go to dinner with friends or to a party or for romantic occasions.

I always put my Cashmere Mist on the same way: I apply it to all the pressure points like the magazines have told me to do—on my wrists, my neck, behind my ears, around my shoulders, and under my boobs. I don't remember what magazine told me to apply it under my boobs, but it doesn't seem to hurt.

Sometimes, if I want to feel extra special, I put it on my legs so I smell extra fantastic, but that's not too often, as I don't like the wet feeling of the lotion on my legs sticking slightly to my pants if I'm wearing them.

I've always gotten compliments on my Cashmere Mist. The guys love it. "You always smell so good," some of them have told me in the past.

The best part about all of it is that no one else who is close to me wears Cashmere Mist. It's all mine. It's my scent, just like the friends and family I've mentioned have their scents.

Coco Chanel once said of perfume, "It is the unseen, unforgettable, ultimate accessory of fashion . . . that heralds your arrival and prolongs your departure." Don't you love that? I could not agree more with Ms. Chanel. It is the sweetened addition to the people we care most about in our lives and the ones who come in briefly and leave that indelible mark.

The Buy

"Will you marry me?"

When you stop to think about it, it's pretty much the most mesmerizing question someone could ever ask.

A person is telling you that they want to spend every day for the rest of their life with you until they die. No matter what your problem is, no matter your little idiosyncrasies, annoying habits, criminal record, or otherwise, that's all fine, they know all about that stuff and they still want to spend the rest of their lives with you until they die. To add to it, they want to get up in front of your friends and family and in front of a religious figure or a judge or anyone legally acceptable to make this promise binding. The search is over. You are the mythical figure they mentioned in conversation "The person I marry . . ." or "I hope to find my soul mate one day. . . ." It's you. You are the one they want to be with until they are no more.

Not only is it a really heavy thing to grasp, but wow, how flattering.

This was what was going through my mind when Pete took out the six-carat emerald-cut diamond engagement ring from Tiffany's and asked for my hand in marriage.

It was a nothing Thursday in 2003. *Friends* was a rerun that night, so earlier that morning I mentioned to Pete that maybe we'd go out to dinner, which he was fine with. No mention of where we'd go had been discussed. Nothing, not even Pete, seemed out of the ordinary. It was a sunny Thursday March day in Southern California, highs were in the low seventies, and I wore a pair of True Religion jeans and a black Co-Op knit cardigan with a white button-down shirt underneath untucked, skimming the tops of my thighs, leaving a nice unpolished, comfortable look for my nothing-out-of-the-ordinary day on the eighth floor at the Promo House offices. Pete wore his usual unordinary attire: a James Perse T-shirt—this one was long sleeve in black—Levi's, and his black Prada driving shoes. I saw him once during the day when he came down to give me a quick kiss hello before he went to lunch, something he normally did. He didn't seem happier to see me, just normal-happy to see his gal.

I got home first that night. Pete told me he was having a quick drink with a screenwriter. I was watching *Entertainment Tonight*. Mary Hart was reporting on the fact that since the war in Iraq had recently begun, stars were planning on dressing down in a more subdued tone for the Oscars that Sunday night. I was taking off my jeans and black sweater for the time being until we were going to dinner, leaving on the white button-down, and throwing on my black Juicy velvet sweats. I watched Bob Goen reporting that Tobey Maguire had signed on to appear in the sequel of *Spider-Man* despite a back injury. My stomach was starting to growl in the middle of the report, so I went down to the kitchen to grab some tortilla chips to tide me over until we went to dinner. As I was eating out of the pantry closet, Pete came home.

He had a really nice smile on his face. He seemed like he was in a really good mood—more than usual, but not enough to take note of as he hugged and kissed me hello and grabbed some chips for himself. I was telling him about the crappy meeting I'd had with a network that didn't like the way we were promoting their shows. I still had my head in the pantry, using a shelf as my table as I opened a jar of salsa and began to dip. I was really hungry, and some chips that hadn't made it to my mouth instead fell on the floor.

"You know, you're adorable," he said and smiled as I was in the middle of telling him about my day. This stopped me in my eating/work-gripe frenzy as I turned to give him a smile full of chips. He kissed me on the cheek.

He had actually mentioned to me a week before that he didn't like the fact that I had a habit of eating a meal out of the refrigerator or from the pantry. That night he thought it was adorable. Men. They can be so finicky sometimes.

I continued to eat my salsa and chips out of the pantry closet and continued to go on about my day.

"The jerks don't want to pay us what they owe us," I told Pete. "That's what's behind this," I said with a mouthful. Just then, I dripped some of the salsa onto my white button-down shirt and let out a pissed-off bellow.

"Son of a bitch!" I shouted as I turned around to grab a paper towel to swipe the salsa off my shirt. These were the last words I would articulate before turning around again and seeing Pete down on one knee with the six-carat emerald-cut diamond engagement ring from Tiffany's.

"I was going to wait until this weekend"—he smiled

brightly—"and I was going to do all this stuff—take you out to a nice place, get some roses, have some guy playing the violin. . . . Seeing you standing there though, I just thought that this was the most appropriate way to ask you. Dean . . . Adena, will you marry me?"

I was numb in my tracks, and yet my senses were on highest alert. I could feel the wet salsa sticking the white button-down shirt to my chest. Some tortilla crumbs were underneath my bare feet. I had a slight wedgie from my boy-cut sheers, and *Entertainment Tonight* was announcing the birthdays of Holly Hunter, Spike Lee, and Carl Reiner.

He wanted to marry *me*. He wanted to spend the rest of his life with *me*. Why me? Who was I to be asked such a question, and with salsa on my white shirt no less? What did I have that the others didn't? Me? Are you sure?

"Are you sure?" I blurted out with this smiling, perplexed look on my face as he remained in place, bent on one knee holding the ring to my face. I took a step forward and another chip speared its way into my foot.

"I want to spend the rest of my life with you," he whispered in that positive, matter-of-fact tone I'd come to love.

Who was I to turn such a thing down?

Was I making too much out of it? Sure, he was asking me to marry him, and this was a huge deal, but billions of other people, even the people closest to me, had been asked this same question and they seemed to take it off the cuff. They went on with their lives, had children, and no one ever mentioned, "I couldn't believe he wanted to marry me."

Still, the thought of the words "I want to spend the rest of my life with you" had me shaking and crying and unable to speak. What a statement. What a beautiful, unselfish, loving, trusting statement.

So I nodded my head and accepted his proposal.

The ring looked incredibly obnoxious on the tiny fourth finger of my left hand. I would have to start getting manicures on a regular basis. "Why did the ring have to be so big?" I thought to myself. "I'll have to drag my arm across the floor. I'll look like the hunchback of Notre Dame with amazing jewelry. I could blind someone with this thing. I'm just going to tell him it's too big." This was what was going through my mind as we kissed madly. "You're out of your mind!" I could hear generations of women in my family screaming. "We've never heard of such a thing. You're upset that the diamond is too big? This should be a problem for you? How did you get into this family?"

"Do you like the ring?" he whispered, admiring it on my finger.

"It's the most beautiful ring I've ever seen," I cried.

"The thing looks like ten carats on you." He laughed, taking my hand. "If I'd known it was going to look so big, I could have gotten you one carat and saved the money."

Relaxed Fit

When you are newly engaged and gearing up to plan a wedding, start prenatal vitamins, have children, and start a new phase in your life, a full-time job—if you can swing it—is out of the question. It just takes up too much time. This was the reasoning that Pete and I had when I quit my job with Promo House.

"There's just too much that has to be done," Pete reasoned, "and your work is going to suffer for it."

"I just feel like I'll be wasting your time," I told my boss. "Even as I'm telling you this, my mind is going back and forth between lemon- or cream-colored napkins for the wedding reception."

The twenty-four-year-olds were ready to sit shivah for me.

"Will you just leave a pair of your shoes here?" Jesse cried. "Just so a part of you is with us."

My co-thirtysomethings thought I was out of my mind.

"Getting ready for a wedding is no reason to give up your

life," Julian scolded. "You are going to hate shopping all day. What are you going to do when the wedding is over?"

"I'll have babies and go to PTA meetings. This part of my life is over," I scolded back. "I've worked my butt off, literally, for the last fifteen years. It's time to do something else."

"That's the thing," Paula said. "You won't be doing anything else. Trust me; first you'll plan your days, but slowly you're going to find yourself watching HBO in the middle of the afternoon. Four o'clock after Oprah is a killer; I know this from maternity leave," she said, clutching her heart. "It's the longest part of life you'll ever experience when you have nothing to do. You'll get to that four o'clock hour one day when it's another four hours from dinner and there's nothing else to do. Take my advice; pray for something good on HBO. That's the best you can hope for."

So I stopped speaking to them until I couldn't take the grief anymore and called up one day, telling them I would freelance whenever they needed me.

The strange phenomenon about quitting or being fired from a job is all those clothes, which are just not needed anymore. There is too much in your closet that just doesn't need be there. All those clothes you bought in order to wear a different outfit each day is now unnecessary, since the same pair of jeans can be worn for months on end. And why not? No one except your loved one sees you on a daily basis.

You know when you find a really good-fitting T-shirt or a pair of pants and you buy five of them in an array of colors? The one T-shirt or pair of pants that you favored over the others is the one that gets worn. The others? Donate them. You're never going to wear them again unless you drop a jar of chocolate syrup on the outfit you normally wear (like I did). When you don't have a job, there aren't enough people in the world who are going to see you wear the same thing twice.

At first you continue to set your alarm to 7 a.m. You jump out of bed with the world as your playground and wonder, "Shall it be the museum today? How about a nice matinee after the gym?" You try to make plans with your stay-at-home-mom girlfriends, but they don't have time for an afternoon matinee or lunch or anything else. There's soccer practice to drive to, ballet lessons, piano lessons, and tutors to tend to. "You'll find that out soon enough," they tell me.

Pretty soon, you realize that the wedding preparations are taking no time at all. Instead of meeting the florist and the cake baker in one day, mix it up. "I'm busy that Monday with the florist," you tell the baker, "Tuesday is better for me."

Pretty soon, the flowers are picked, the cake is decided on, it's too much of a pain to drive to the gym and, before you know it, Paula's prediction comes true. You find yourself sitting in front of the television at four in the afternoon in the same shirt and pants you've been wearing for the last five days, and you're ticked off because there's nothing on HBO.

So you clean out your closet . . . for the tenth time.

Tradition

Heidi was twenty-six when she got engaged. The engagement party was a Sunday-morning brunch, and Serena and I went shopping with her. She decided on a dress from Bebe in white with red cherries on it. We looked everywhere for shoes, and we finally found the perfect pair in white with red piping on them at the Macy's in the Century City Mall. You'd never seen an outfit more put-together. The shoes and dress were like a match made in perfect-for-a-daytime-engagement-brunch heaven. The only problem was, the shoes were $500—more than our weekly paycheck at the time. Serena and I took a huddle and wondered if we might all pitch in for them together and make the shoes her engagement present. That's when a sneaky woman, though not sneaky-looking at all, more like a mom in her mid-fifties with a pink sweatsuit on, whispered to us as the salesman walked away. "Pssst, tape 'em up and return them after you wear them," she said.

"What? What do you mean 'tape 'em up'?" Serena and I inquired.

"You put Scotch tape on the bottom of the shoes, and then you can walk all over the place and not scuff them up. Take the tape off afterward, and the heels are like new."

This was the smartest thing that Serena and I had ever heard. Heidi thought so too when we told her.

"Are you sure they don't scuff?" Heidi inquired.

"I've been doing it for years," the woman said as she handed a pair of Yves Saint Laurent black pumps to a salesman. "I'll take them," she said, winking at us.

It was worth a try, and they did look perfect with the dress. . . . We decided to go for the crime.

At the engagement brunch, everyone loved Heidi's outfit. "Those shoes are perfect," guests told her as she winked at us.

After the brunch, Serena and I went back to Heidi's apartment, where we carefully took off the now-soiled tape. Underneath it was a gorgeous, spotless heel. The problem now was the grief in bringing the shoes back. Should we go back to the same Macy's in the Century City Mall? Maybe bring them to the Macy's at the Beverly Center?

"No," I said creating the perfect crime, "let's bring them to the Macy's in Westwood. No one goes there." Which they didn't, and the Macy's in Westwood closed soon afterward.

Then Heidi got a pang of fear.

"I can't go. I can't do it," she cried. "You do it."

"Why should I do it?" I countered. "They're your shoes."

"Technically, they're Macy's."

"No, technically, they're yours, and soon half of mine," Heidi's fiancé Eric announced to us as he entered the conversation.

"You do it, Serena," we said.

"Are you crazy?" She winced. "I'm not doing that."

"Would Shawn do it?" Heidi asked, meaning Serena's fiancé.

"Shawney?" Serena cooed on the phone. "Would you return a pair of shoes for Heidi?"

We never heard an answer.

"This is stupid," Eric said as he grabbed the box of shoes. "I'll return them."

We watched Eric go on his way, and the three of us went back to sorting Heidi's engagement gifts. An hour later, Eric came home. His face was white.

"They knew you taped them," he said. "You made me feel like a criminal!"

Thoughts of the woman in Macy's, the day of the crime, came into our heads. Could this have been a setup?

"They finally took them back after I made them believe I had no idea what they were talking about, but don't ever do that again." He sighed, going into the bedroom and shutting the door.

We never taped shoes again. The fear of returning them scared us out of a life of crime.

When Serena got engaged to Shawn that same year, after hours', days', and weeks' worth of shopping, Serena bought a cream-colored suit jacket with a matching skirt.

"Go to my tailor," I told Serena. "She's really good." She was. I really liked that tailor and took all of my clothes to her. Unfortunately, she closed down at some point through the years and I had to switch, but this was long before that happened.

"SHE SHORTENED THE SKIRT TO MY ASS!" Serena called, yelling at me. "SHE RUINED MY OUTFIT!"

I hopped into my car immediately and sped over to Serena's apartment, where I found her practically comatose.

"It's not that bad," Shawn kept saying over and over, trying to calm her down.

"I like the length," I told her.

Truthfully, the skirt was way too short—tragically short—but I'd never let her know until now. She's always had an amazing body, so it really didn't make that much of a difference. Had I told the truth at the time, though, the whole engagement party and possibly the wedding would have been canceled. I had forgotten the whole reason I went to that tailor in the first place. Serena's engagement took place during my short-skirt era, when I liked having my clothes shortened to the ass. Maybe I was the tailor's only happy customer and that's why she had to go out of business.

Ten years after these stories became dinner-party fodder, it was finally my turn to find the engagement outfit, and I did not want Lina coming with us.

"She knows what fits you," Pete complained.

"It's a sacred thing!" I told him. "Parties and benefits are one thing; this is something close friends do together."

"That's the dumbest thing I've ever heard," he reasoned. "Don't you want to look good? Don't you want to be a show-stopper at your engagement party?"

Of course I wanted to be a showstopper; of course I wanted to be the greatest-looking engaged woman that ever got engaged. But tradition was tradition.

"Tradition is tradition!" I yelled.

"At least let her come with you!" he said.

It was like taking your little sister with you if you ever had one—your 5'6", obnoxious, opinionated, glass-is-half-empty, thinks-she-knows-you-better-than-you-know-yourself, tells-everyone-in-hearing-distance-that-you-have-no-ass (and how *thank God* she got you out of those stripper heels) little sister, and the only thing you can do is give her the finger behind her back every time she turns around.

"I love it!" Heidi said as she whipped out her boob to breast-feed her latest newborn.

"It's perfect!" Serena said, beaming.

"Ladies and gentlemen," Lina said sulkily about my white Costume National pantsuit, "Casper the Friendly Ghost is now a fashion statement."

"The hippos are in full bloom," she said of the flowered Eduardo Lucero floor-length dress.

"If you can wear her dresses," she said of another designer, "then you know she's marketing to the masses now."

I looked over at the girls.

"If you don't do it, I will," Serena mouthed.

"If I didn't have a child attached to my breast, I'd knock her to the ground," Heidi vowed.

We knew what had to be done, and I wanted to be the one to do it.

"Lina, could I speak to you privately for just a second?" I asked her politely.

"Oh, the bride is getting nervous," she said, smirking at my closest friends. "Every bride bitches me out by now."

"No, I'm not turning into a bitch," I calmly said, "but I think that you are."

"Look, the truth hurts," Lina said with a laugh. "If you can't take it, I don't have to stay."

"OK, then, thanks for everything and good luck," I said peacefully.

"Pete isn't going to like this."

"I'll deal with my fiancé, thank you," I told her.

"Good luck," she said, giving my body the last once-over she'd ever give. "And I really mean that." Then she walked out of the store.

Five minutes later, I had purchased the white Costume National pantsuit.

And we all loved it, except for Pete.

"What's the matter with you?" he screamed at me, standing in the driveway in his Banjo-fur sweater when the girls and I drove up to my home with smiles on our faces.

"What are you talking about?" I asked, getting out of the car.

"Ladies," he tried to say calmly, though it was obvious he was not, "I need to speak with Adena. Can she call you later?"

We all had nervous smiles on our faces, unable to decide what to do.

"Ladies, really, I'm very upset right now and I really need to speak with her, so if you could . . . ?"

Heidi and Serena scurried into Heidi's car, still nervously smiling at me, me nervously smiling back, wishing I could have gotten into the car with them. I mouthed, *"I'll call you,"* as I walked into the house.

"You had no right to fire Lina! You call her up right now and apologize!" Pete yelled as I stepped inside.

I started laughing, really laughing, with this statement. He was being ridiculous.

"I'm serious, Adena. I am so mad at you right now, I can't even look at you!"

I had never seen Pete with such anger in his face. He was not the matter-of-fact Pete I knew. He was angry Pete, Pete the angry man, and even though I could not take him seriously, I knew I had to at least put up a front.

"I had to fire her," I told him calmly. "She was completely out of line. She was saying the most awful things. I just felt it was the right thing to do."

"Well, it wasn't the right thing to do. She's done amazing

things with you. Do you know how much better you've looked since she started picking out your clothes?"

"And what's that supposed to mean?" I said, raising my voice.

"When I met you, I was embarrassed by how you looked!"

Hold back.

I took a deep breath. Was he right? Had a professional come in and made me look the way I always wanted to look? Did I really look that bad before and didn't know it? Was he right? Was he right? Was I wrong? Did I really look that bad before?

"Did I really look that bad before?"

"Yes! You really looked that bad before!"

That was the worst put-down of all.

"So why are you with me?"

"Don't start that chick shit!" he yelled, handing me the phone. "Just call her right now and apologize, and I don't want to hear another thing about it!" Then he went into his home office and slammed the door.

I didn't call Lina. I didn't do anything for a good five minutes. I sat in our foyer and looked at the plastic suit holder that held my engagement outfit. I stared at it and stared at it, unable to think of what to do next.

And then, I left the suit where it was and I walked out the door, slamming it as loud as I could.

Thanks for Being There

Esther and Frank, my mother's parents, both died suddenly when I was eleven years old. I was at sleep-away camp for eight weeks and came home to find them gone. I loved them so much, and I didn't get to say good-bye. They weren't sick when I left. It was all very sudden. There had been a funeral and everyone cried together and no one told me. My brother David told me that for five days, the house was wall to wall with people coming to pay their respects. My brother Michael said he clocked it at three hundred people, but David said he thought it felt more like four hundred. I've always had a bit of contempt with the family for overlooking me. I suppose, though, when two people you love most in this world die suddenly, nothing makes sense.

I really should have known as soon as I walked in the door of our house. They weren't there like they always were. Esther wasn't sitting at the kitchen table sipping iced coffee and gossiping with my mother and fanning herself with a scrap piece of paper she'd found nearby. Her signature costume jewelry cocktail rings and layers of gold necklaces weren't swaying back and forth as she went on and on about this one's heart attack, that one's business that failed, who wore what to the party and what were they thinking, and yelling at my poor dad that the house was still too hot even though he'd already put the air conditioning down to sixty-five degrees. Frank wasn't sitting outside on our porch under the yellow-and-white-striped awning, immaculately dressed on a hot August day without a bead of sweat, relaxing in a pair of seersucker pants and pristine white golf shirt, transistor radio in hand, earpiece in ear, listening to the Phillies game, drowning out my grandmother's nonstop chatter. Their best friends, my Aunt Ruth and Uncle Lou Goldman *were* there however.

"Tell her," my dad told my mom.

"They left us," my mom cried.

"Why didn't anyone tell me?" I asked.

No one had an answer.

Life went on as usual that day, minus Esther and Frank. I seemed to be the only one who realized it though. Everyone had already cried together and gone on with their lives and I didn't get to say good-bye. A tray of corned beef and turkey sandwiches, cole slaw, and cold french fries with cheese from Hymie's Deli was sitting on the kitchen table. We all consumed it, all except for the eternally size-six Arlene, dressed in a classic linen taupe-colored button-down top and matching linen pants that suddenly looked way too big on her.

Sometime later that day, I found myself in my mother's closet. Hanging on a hanger was one of Esther's favorite outfits, a coral knit top and matching skirt that she said of herself when she wore it, "I make all the other ladies feel drab when they see me in this." I took the outfit in my arms and breathed in the scent of Esther's floral and Aqua Net hair spray aroma. I snuck back the next day and the day after that and the day after that until the trace of scent had morphed into a bouquet of my mother's own Chloé perfume (Arlene's signature scent of that time) and Ban roll-on. After that, I pretended Esther and Frank were in Florida with all the other grandparents.

After we cleaned out their apartment, the clothing and jewelry arrived. It was said that one of Frank's darkest days was when his accounting firm moved from downtown Philadelphia into the Main Line suburbs. No more shopping on his lunch hour. He must have found a way, however, since there were more than two dozen tailor-made shirts that were still in their boxes, never opened. There were so many gold bracelets, rings, faux diamond brooches, pearls, and earrings (all clip-ons) that it was too much to go over. My mother dumped it all in a large drawer. I wore one of Esther's watches, a white plastic band with a black timepiece, for over a year. It never worked. Neither the grandmother nor the granddaughter bothered to put a battery in it. What was the point? Let someone else keep time and let us know when we had to be there.

Twenty-five years later, only one of the tailored boxed shirts remains downstairs in the basement closet of my parents' house, never opened, along with a forest green suit with Frank's initials embroidered on the inside pocket. That costume jewelry is still in that same drawer. Every now and then I go fishing through it and find some sort of treasure—a long strand of faux pearls with the paint chipping off, a plastic beaded necklace that looks like real onyx as long as you don't get too close. Whenever my cousin Michele's nine-year-old daughter Rachel comes over, she always picks something from the drawer as a special treat. Last time, it was a silver dollar spraypainted gold that was glued onto a gold backing and hanging on a gold chain—all faux of course, except for the dollar. I keep one piece of Esther's jewelry in my own home. It's a small gold (real for a change) umbrella charm with a diamond raindrop dripping from the side, and a gold chain. My mother and her sister, my Aunt Maxine, had given it to Esther for Mother's Day one year and she never took it off. I won't tell you where I keep it in my house. If it gets stolen or lost, I swear I'll jump out a window I'll be so upset. I only wear it for special occasions and think the same thought when I put it on each time: Esther would have hated to miss a good party.

That coral knit sweater and matching skirt still hangs in my mother's closet. It's the last outfit hanging on the left side on a plastic yellow hanger. Rather than placing the sweater to drape over the hanger with the skirt underneath, my mom has both articles side by side on the hanger. Whenever I come across it, I give it a touch and feel the fabric.

I just wanted you to know that I've missed you so much all these years.

There have been so many times when I wished that you were here.

In a way though, I know you always have been.

On the Surface

spent the next four days at Felicia's house. Pete called and e-mailed nonstop about how the gardener mowed over the beautiful tulips I'd planted and how he had fired him over it. He called to remind me that it was time for my car's three-month oil change. He called to remind me I had a dentist appointment and offered to bring over my toothbrush when he noticed I didn't have it.

On the fourth day, a package arrived. It was a pair of the highest heels I'd ever seen, cushioned in broken pieces of tortilla chips. Felicia and I measured the heel and laughed when we saw that it was a record ten inches. The note on the gift said *"I miss everything about you."*

So I went home to my fiancé.

"Don't ever do that to me again," he cried as we embraced.

We never talked about what he'd said to me, but it resonated every time I looked in my closet for something to wear. I saw Pete cringe in the slightest way when I went to grab my Theory khaki suit pants. Maybe he wasn't cringing over my Theory pants. I mean, what could possibly be wrong with a pair of Theory suit pants in khaki? In retrospect, his bad back might have flared up for a second or he suddenly remembered that he forgot something at the office. He didn't mention what the cringe was about though, so I could only suspect the cringe was over my choice in clothing. When I got ready to go the gym, I thought first about throwing on my gray cotton drawstring pants that I'd previously dropped some bleach on in a laundry mishap, but instead put on a pair of black wide-leg leggings and a matching black sports bra. He looked at me a little longer, maybe a half a second longer than he should have and it made me wonder. Was what I was wearing OK to work out in? Would someone recognize me at the gym and tell their friends, "I saw Pete Rodgers's fiancée at the gym perfectly matched. I would have looked for the stick up her ass, but my Yoga boogie jazzercise class was starting." Or worse, "I saw poor Pete Rodgers's fiancée at the gym looking like such a schlep. I guess Pete's going for the plain-Jane type now." I had bought a new pair of pants and hadn't been able to shorten them in time for an event we were going to and had no choice but to put on a pair of six-inch heels to make up for the extra fabric. You couldn't even see the shoes under the pants, but I could tell by Pete's quiet demeanor in the car that this was no good . . . I think. Would he be embarrassed to be seen with me? I did notice that he didn't introduce me to someone he said hello to. Maybe he didn't know their name. I would never know, but would always wonder. So many questions to ask, so many petty arguments to get into before we could find a common ground. Any self-respecting woman wouldn't have given two beans about what he thought, but I wasn't at that point yet. Remember, I loved him and he loved me. He had even formally asked me to spend the rest of his life with him and had sealed my answer with a way-oversized-for-my-small-hand (not that I'm complaining) six-carat emerald-cut diamond ring from Tiffany's on my now perpetually manicured hand. Again, any self-respecting person would have just asked if everything was all right. It would take a little more time until I reached that breaking point. In short, I did not want to rock the boat. And I was, as I had been once before in my life, willing to spend the next fifty years vying for a nice, clean sail.

And then the tsunami struck again.

We were getting ready to go to yet another benefit and I bought what I thought, what the saleswomen thought, what the saleswomen at the store next to the store I bought the outfit at thought, and what the Five thought when I went to each and every one of their homes with it, was a fantastic outfit. I had gorgeous shoes—four inches, a compromise—and, of course, my ring. I had spent the entire day at the hair salon, got my makeup done, a pedicure, a manicure, and various waxing that no one would ever notice but I did just to be on the safe side. I looked stylish, gorgeous, and I did it all myself. Pete said nothing, but he didn't cringe or pause when he saw me. He simply said, "Great, ready to go?" As we walked out to get into the car, he turned to me in that matter-of-fact way and said, "I guess this is the best you'll ever be able to do by yourself."

I said nothing as I got into the car. My mind, however, was racing a mile a minute, as was my anger.

Who the heck was this guy? Who the heck was he to judge? That's when his wardrobe choices came into my head. Weren't there any other colors in the world to wear besides black, gray, and white? And no, to make up for this bland blunder, red corduroy pants with a bright yellow T-shirt that screams Ronald

McDonald are not the answer. Hey, here's an idea! How about some browns? And, by the way, a little pink would not make someone look as "swishy" as one might think.

Tighty whities that sagged in the ass. With all the talk about my underwear, Pete wore tighty whities. To be completely honest, I couldn't have cared less what he wore under his jeans. Pete's tighty-whitie underwear would never have been an issue for me had I not been told that my underwear was "for fourth-graders." What I'm saying is, if you're going to try to change someone else's undergarment comfort for your own stimulating delights, do you really think that "Give it to me, big boy" is the first thing I'll think of when I see those saggy drawers of yours coming at me?

And one more thing, I get the idea of mourning over a dog that has passed away. I've never actually had a dog, but I fully respect the love and care that a relationship with a dog over the years can bring to a person and I completely understand that, when taken away, the blow is right up there with losing a member of one's family. Having said that, however, having your dearly departed bichon frise's excess dog hair woven into a sweater is beyond any code of fashion, or ethics for that matter, that I could think of. Worse, wearing the sweater in public on numerous occasions. Worse than that, wearing the sweater on a rainy day, causing the smell of wet dog fur to become a call of the wild, inviting packs of dogs to come running from every direction within smelling distance to attack even the fiancée standing next to the person wearing the mordant item.

This was where my breaking point began to surface. I was literally starting to get sick of the sight of him. I could not even stand to be so close to him in the car.

Now, I could have freaked out on him, I could have told him all those things I was thinking in my head, but I didn't. I could have jumped out of the car and walked the five miles back to the house in my dress and heels, but who was that going to punish? He was just not worth it, and there was no way I was going to start to cry and ruin my makeup for someone who didn't deserve another ounce of my energy. I may not have had an ass, but I had just grown a backbone.

We went to the benefit and I smiled and laughed and talked the talk and walked the walk of a lady who, for the very first time in her life, absolutely loved the way she looked—inside and out. The compliments abounded.

"I've never seen you look more beautiful," someone said.

"Being in love agrees with you," another person said.

"Did you get work done?" one more person asked.

As we got in the car to leave, Pete turned to me and said, "I didn't think you looked so great, but evidently everyone else did. I guess I was wrong," he said, leaning over and giving me a kiss on the cheek.

After we got home and I watched him hang up his coat, he turned to me and held out his arms to hug me. I did not come to him.

"Pete," I said in the most matter-of-fact of ways, "I wanna break up."

I told him it wouldn't work in one of those crushing conversations where everyone cries and no one leaves happy, and you start to second-guess yourself but know that somehow it will all be fine in the end.

And it was.

It is.

Of course, I went through a terrible mourning period. I lost ten pounds over the breakup. . . . OK, seven of those pounds was the ring (not that I'm complaining).

The Makeover

When you break up with someone, there's never just one reason. It's never just because you caught him with three hookers in a motel room in downtown L.A., smoking crack (I didn't; I'm just trying to make a point). It's never just because you hate his mother or his sister or his best friend (which I didn't, again making a point). I certainly didn't break up with Pete just because he was so insecure about himself that he threw it on me and my wardrobe choices. There are a million underlying reasons you are breaking up that add up to the ultimate decision to go separate ways. When people ask you what happened, though, something like finding your fiancé with three hookers smoking crack in a downtown L.A. motel seems like it would be such a wonderful cut-and-dried answer.

If only life were that simple.

The Five advised me to tell people, "It just didn't work out," which I found to be a really bad excuse. That flippant statement causes tons of questions like, "Why didn't it work out?" "Couldn't you work it out?" and, my favorite, "There must have been something that made you break up with him; you can't just say that it didn't work out."

So what am I supposed to say?

"We broke up because he couldn't decide if he loved or hated the fact that I had a habit of not closing cabinet doors or eating a meal off of a shelf in the pantry"?

"I called off the engagement because he despised the delight I took in wearing cotton underwear"?

"I took back my established affirmation of spending the rest of my life with him because I felt that he cared more about the depleting ozone layer than he did the people closest to him"?

"I canceled the engagement because I didn't feel comfortable getting dressed in the morning for fear I was wearing the wrong thing"?

"I gave Pete back the ring because it was getting to the point where someone would ask me how I was and I'd answer, 'Let me ask Pete just to make sure' "?

"You know what? He just didn't love me for me and in return, I could never love him."

I needed to go home to Philadelphia. I needed to get away from Los Angeles, away from Pete, away from my life, and get back to the womb until I could sort things out and see where my head was.

I slept the first day, ate everything in my parents' house on the second day, and had calmed down enough the third day to get ready to go out with my family for a nice dinner.

I was sitting with my mother in her room, gabbing with her as she started to get dressed. She had her hair in curlers, no makeup on yet; she was wearing a mundane nude-colored bra and the only non-classic piece of clothing she owns—an old pink tattered chenille robe that I think she's been wearing since I was ten. She was sitting on the edge of her bed as we spoke, leaning over as she crouched down to put her feet into some panty hose. From my point of observation, I noticed a slight middle-age spread. In other words, this was not her best look. Just then, my dad walked into the room. He looked at her and then he looked at me and then he smiled this admiring grin. "You know something?" He beamed. "Your mother is the most beautiful woman in the world."

Now, I'm not one of those people who thinks that their parents are the most romantic couple there ever was. This couple could have been anyone; it just happened to have been my parents. Married for forty-five years, they have a beautiful relationship, and as much as I admire them for it, I don't want to base my own life on it. I want my own love story and not a carbon copy of someone else's. It goes back to the lesson I learned when I tried to be Madonna in high school: Never try to perpetrate the whole look; just go for the little nuances. As my father leaned over to give my mother a kiss and she shooed him away, laughing playfully then finally allowing him to give her a peck on the cheek, I knew that I had made the right decision.

Deep down in my heart, I knew that Pete wasn't the one thing I knew for certain. There was always the possibility of a beautiful boy who could see through everything. It did matter to Pete how I looked and what I wore. He loved parts of me; there was no doubt about that. He wanted a creation of his own, though, and it was way too late. I already had my story.

As I head into my late thirties, I am a single woman, but that doesn't begin to define who I am. I will love again. Someone will love me again. I will wear six-inch heels until I don't want to wear them anymore. (But I'm correcting myself even as I write this. They're going to have to bury me with those shoes on.) I will continue to buy Gilligan & O'Malley underwear from Target until they change the formula and I am forced to look elsewhere. I will also wear Cosabella and Hanro and La Perla underwear and push-up bras and maybe even some padded underwear if I feel my butt looks too flat. I'll make those decisions when the mood strikes. I will ask a friend's opinion about a blouse, pants, or skirt and add it into my final analysis instead of allowing it be the set answer. I will wear everything from the Gap to Galliano, and it will never be about price, it will always be about how it makes me feel. I might still lie about my prom dress. That's my prerogative.

Maybe the key to it all lies in something my buddy Oprah once said: "Life is bigger than just buying shoes . . . but shoes are very important." Maybe it's written in one of my friend Madonna's songs: "Express yourself so you can respect yourself." Maybe though, it's even more than that.

Tucked inside the fibers and buttons and pockets is the story of our lives, the lessons we learn, the people we love. For me, it's my awkwardness clumsily stitched into a pair of split Dolphin shorts, a prom dress, some oversize boxer shorts, a pair of deep blue Pumas with a yellow swoosh. An eighteen-year-old girl's feelings for her first love linger inside an old 8-ball jacket sitting in the back of a grown man's closet. My feminine sexpot fumes through some halter tops and cigarette pants, wherever they may be. The insecurities of a thirty-year-old woman are concealed inside some old Hugo Boss suits, just wishing they could break free. The enduring influence of a coral knit skirt and top followed by a long row of classic eternally size-six women's suits and jackets are in a closet in Philadelphia, reminding me of the exuberance for life, dignity, and self-respect those two women have taught me by example. My confidence and grace is first in my self-knowledge and second in my clothing—the haute designers who make me feel dazzling, the cheap Lycra flower dresses that bonded me to the dearest friends I would ever know. My faith is in my future. It shines through a white Vera Wang gown matched with a lace veil that I have yet to see firsthand, but know by heart.

That's my love story . . . so far.

Acknowledgments

To those for whom I wear my heart on my sleeve ... my deepest appreciation ...

To Erin Moore, editor extraordinaire, the magnificent EM, Goddess of the Edit for whom I am most grateful. Thank you for your passionate support, expert opinions, and, most of all, our marathon heart-to-heart tête-à-têtes. It has been the luckiest coup to have you as my editor.

To Gotham publisher Bill Shinker for this incredible opportunity. This experience has been the time of my life (figuratively and literally) and my gratitude is beyond measure.

To my brilliant agent, Brian DeFiore, who got the joke. B, my respect for you is enormous, my debt to you is bigger than any Barneys bill I could ever receive.

To Eric Brooks, one of my dearest friends who, thank God, also happens to be the best entertainment attorney in Hollywood.

You have gone above and beyond and I thank you for always looking out for me.

To Leslie Jane Seymour, editor in chief of *Marie Claire* magazine, for whom I am beyond grateful. With my deepest respect and gratitude, thank you for believing in my work.

To all my buddies at *Marie Claire* including Patti Adcroft, Fan Winston, and Nicole Brown.

A huge thank-you to all the faithful readers of *Marie Claire* magazine.

And without a doubt to my fairy god-sister, Susan Swimmer, for whom I could go on and on and on. If it wasn't for your kindness, determination, and keen eye, this book would still be on my computer. You are the truest friend and a sister in my heart.

To my scribe allies and gym rat cohorts Timothy Gray, Steve Chagollan, and Ted Johnson from *Daily Variety* for the many years of props.

For the valuable advice, help, and welfare, thank you Kate Garrick, Jessica Sindler, Lloyd Bucher, Julian Hooper, Leslie Meyers, Michael Minden, Jake Tapper, Liz Ziemska, Elana Barry; thank you to Helena, the newly appointed seventh, for allowing me to be an honorary WBTV office member; big thanks to Richie Schwartz.

To Ian Kerner, my brother from another mother and advice guru, for his treasure trove of support.

To those who allowed me to spill the Dior, my touchstones: I-My, Heides, Ree, Fels, Ray, and Suz, and to the Granola Man and all the paramours mentioned who remain in my heart with cherished affection.

To my brood: cousin Michele, sister-in-law Samantha, brother Michael, bonus mother Elaine, and to my brother David who puts the hysterical in Halpern.

And finally, to those who have inspired, adorned, and are

simply adored: Madonna, Oprah Winfrey, Donna Karan and Vera Wang, Barneys New York, Bloomingdale's, Saks Fifth Avenue, Macy's, Lord & Taylor, Diavolina and XTC Shoes for six-inch heels, the genius designers of Target's Gillian & O'Malley underwear, and in loving memory of Bonwit Teller, Strawbridge & Clothier, John Wanamaker's, and the Birdcage restaurant.